Protecting Your Family Child Care Business

Other Redleaf Press books by Sharon Woodward

Family Child Care Curriculum: Teaching through Quality Care, Second Edition

Family Child Care Curriculum Family Companion

Family Child Care Curriculum Developmental Assessment

By Sharon Woodward and Donna C. Hurley

The Home Visitor's Manual: Tools and Strategies for Effective Interactions with Family Child Care Providers

Family Child Care Guide to Visits, Inspections, and Interviews

PROTECTING
Your Family Child Care Business

Preventing and Addressing Regulatory Challenges

SHARON WOODWARD

Redleaf Press®
www.redleafpress.org
800-423-8309

Published by Redleaf Press
10 Yorkton Court
St. Paul, MN 55117
www.redleafpress.org

First edition 2025
Cover design by Danielle Carnito
Cover photographs by New Africa—stock.adobe.com; curto—stock.adobe.com
Interior design by Douglas Schmitz
Typeset in Freight
Printed in the United States of America
31 30 29 28 27 26 25 24   1 2 3 4 5 6 7 8

Library of Congress Cataloging-in-Publication Data

Names: Woodward, Sharon, author.
Title: Protecting your family child care business : preventing and
   addressing regulatory challenges / Sharon Woodward.
Description: St. Paul, MN : Redleaf Press, [2025] | Includes index. |
   Summary: "Protect your family child care business from licensing issues.
   Respected family child care consultant Sharon Woodward brings years of
   regulation and policy experience to help you protect your family child
   care business-your livelihood and the heart of your home"— Provided by
   publisher.
Identifiers: LCCN 2024018622 (print) | LCCN 2024018623 (ebook) | ISBN
   9781605548371 (paperback) | ISBN 9781605548388 (ebook)
Subjects: LCSH: Family day care. | Child care services.
Classification: LCC HQ778.5 .W66 2025 (print) | LCC HQ778.5 (ebook) | DDC
   362.71/2--dc23/eng/20240514
LC record available at https://lccn.loc.gov/2024018622
LC ebook record available at https://lccn.loc.gov/2024018623

Printed on acid-free paper.

To my beautiful grandson, Max, and to my very special mom, Frances—
two of my greatest inspirations. Thank you!

CONTENTS

ACKNOWLEDGMENTS

I WOULD LIKE TO ACKNOWLEDGE my editor at Redleaf Press, Melissa York, for her direction and collaboration in producing this book. I don't believe I could have done this without her.

I also wish to acknowledge all the wonderful family child care providers who have opened their homes and shared their stories with me. I am sincerely in awe of all of you.

To all the organizations and agencies that have allowed me the opportunity to provide training to their members throughout the United States—a special thank you to Alejandra Tejeda, Service Employees International Union (SEIU), Inez Chillous, United Federation of Teachers, and Bonnie Caldwell, Civil Service Employees Association (CSEA).

Last but not least, thanks go to my family. To my children, Jenn and Phil, Jamie and Tito, and my son, Michael, who have always been supportive and patient with their outspoken mother/mother-in-law. To my husband, Paul, and my nephew, Martin, who make me laugh and always make me appreciate how lucky I am to have them in my life. To my mother, Frances, who passed away this year at ninety-five, my most wonderful critic. And to my grandchildren Will and Madison, and to my grandson, Max, who inspires me to hope for good things for the future for all children and families.

Thank you all!

I WROTE THIS BOOK BECAUSE I believe strongly in the value of family child care. Having worked as both a provider and a licensor, I remain convinced there are many common objectives shared by both professions. It's hard, however, to ignore the increasing number of providers who have decided to close their programs. Those numbers were magnified during the COVID-19 pandemic. My concern is how many providers will choose to remain closed. I have spoken with too many providers who feel it's just too hard to stay open.

We know what began for many individuals as a simple and often informal arrangement between a family and a provider has significantly changed. There was a time when mothers of young children became licensed so they could stay at home with their own children. It was seen as a temporary way to make a little extra money, caring for relatives or children in the neighborhood while still being at home. For many other providers, family child care was seen as a stepping stone to something else. These individuals were interested in eventually opening child care centers or moving into employment in a related field. Family child care was not acknowledged as a profession, but that has changed.

Most licensed family child care providers are now faced with extensive regulatory requirements. The required investment of time and money as well as expanded regulations, and in many cases higher training and educational requirements for maintaining a license, have significantly changed the picture. Unannounced visits, criminal background checks, fingerprinting, and increased visibility in your community are only a small example of the magnifying glass you and your business are under. That does not mean there aren't individuals who choose to open a family child care program on a time-limited basis. However, that population is much smaller than it was in the past. If you are planning on operating a family child care program, briefly or long term, it is important to clearly understand what you're getting into!

A common message often communicated to providers is that if "they just follow the rules" they will never have complaints, incidents, or issues. My experience has been that this is simply not true. Any small business owner who operates an early child care program (no matter their number of degrees, years of experience, licensing history, or credentials) can, at any time, find their license and their ability to care for children in jeopardy. This can occur, and does occur, in too many avoidable instances.

This book was written to help providers avoid licensing issues. It provides relevant information to help you protect and professionalize your business. A common misconception is that if a complaint is filed or an incident or issue occurs, providers can do little to protect themselves. Many providers become so disillusioned that they "voluntarily" close their programs. As you will find, providers can actually do a great deal to proactively avoid the potential damage that may occur as a result of licensing intervention.

For ease of use, this book has been divided into three sections. Section 1 offers a variety of tools and strategies you can proactively employ in your family child care environment. Acknowledging that problematic issues can happen in professionally run programs is important but sometimes difficult. It's no surprise that many providers find themselves totally unprepared when something unexpected occurs. Section 1 introduces targeted, proactive strategies to help you avoid unintended events that can result in licensing intervention.

Section 2 provides important information to support and assist you if you do find yourself in trouble. This section addresses a variety of issues that may occur as a result of monitoring visits, citations, incidents, and complaint investigations. It also includes important information about your right to appeal negative determinations. You need to know that a large number of providers survive citations, allegations, and investigations, and many win at appeal hearings. Section 2 also provides you with information and support designed to help you navigate your state's regulatory system. This information is designed to help you make an informed decision about how you choose to proceed. Yes, you do have options!

Section 3 demonstrates how providers can withstand licensing intervention and go on to operate successful early child care programs. This section offers information for all providers who want to reinvent or reinvigorate an existing program or open a new program. The early child care profession is becoming increasingly competitive and is constantly changing. This section offers instruction about how to prepare for what may come next. You will find important information about rebuilding enrollment and implementing positive interactive communication with your child care families. Coming back from a licensing intervention can in many instances be more difficult than when you initially applied for your license. Section 3 provides support and instruction for moving forward in a positive and productive way.

The intention of this book is to offer a road map for sustainability in a very challenging profession. You will find remedies and support if and when you do find yourself in trouble. Most importantly, it provides a framework for building back better to achieve a stable and sustainable business. I am hopeful you will find this information helpful, and I sincerely hope it becomes a useful tool in the day-to-day operation of your successful early child care business.

Best,

Sharon

HOW TO CREATE A PROACTIVE PROGRAM

FROM THE FEDERAL GOVERNMENT RIGHT DOWN to states and municipalities, early child care has become a hot topic. A growing number of people realize that you need to have a robust early child care community to maintain a viable workforce, which has led to more officials in the federal and state government taking a closer look at the existing child care system.

This is happening when many family child care providers I have spoken to feel the narrative defining their specific category of care no longer belongs to them. Many family child care providers have been led to believe that there is only one option if they want to receive positive recognition in their profession. They have come to assume that the infrastructure that defines child care centers, structured preschools, and institutionalized settings is the only appropriate model of care available to them.

Why is this relevant information in your attempt to protect and professionalize your program? While it's true that as a provider you are part of a larger profession, which is subject to licensure and regulation, you do have choices about how you structure your program. A critical step in protecting your business is your ability to feel confident in the type of child care you provide. Understanding and appreciating the advantages of managing a family child care environment, where you can develop meaningful relationships while introducing personalized daily routines, will help you feel confident and better able to protect your business.

Feeling confident is a good first step. An important second step is understanding that licensing authorities often find the regulatory oversight of family child care programs especially challenging. Licensing someone's business that is located in a commercial or institutionalized space is distinctly different from licensing a business located in someone's home. The interaction between licensors and providers can be misinterpreted. What is often intended as professional oversight can frequently be interpreted as personal criticism or judgment. The interaction between licensors and providers can become complicated. The following information was developed to help you successfully navigate this process.

I. Case Study One

Anne has been licensed for eleven years. Anne is proud of her business. She currently has a license for six children but hopes to increase her enrollment with the help of her new assistant. For eleven years, Anne has maintained a good relationship with her licensor. She has never received a complaint, and no major licensing issues have come up during monitoring visits. Anne has heard stories about other providers, but she's confident that providers who find themselves in trouble usually deserve it. Occasionally Anne hears grumbling about new regulations, but she's too busy with her full enrollment to investigate what's going on. It's been a long time since she has taken a look at her regulations, but her program is operating smoothly, and if there's something she should know, she's sure her licensor will update her.

One morning after the children arrived and Anne had just finished serving breakfast, she glanced out her front window to see two adults she did not recognize walking toward her front door. Because she needed to get back into the kitchen where the children were finishing up, she waved her visitors around to the other door, anticipating they were selling something and she could easily turn them away.

As Anne passed through the kitchen, she glanced around the room. Her assistant was not due to arrive for another forty-five minutes. Her kitchen was a mess from the breakfast preparation. Breakfast was usually hectic because her own children ate before leaving for school, and immediately after, Anne was left preparing breakfast for the children in her program. The eight-month-old twins Anne cared for had fallen asleep in the playpen, where she had placed them while she served breakfast. She actually felt a little embarrassed opening the door because she had breakfast food on her sweatshirt, and she had yet to comb her hair or brush her teeth. "Oh well," Anne thought, "let me deal with this inconvenient interruption, and then I can get organized."

Much to Anne's surprise, when she opened the door she was greeted by two women who introduced themselves as representatives from her licensing agency. One woman introduced herself as Anne's new licensor. The second woman introduced herself as the licensing supervisor. Anne was stunned. She informed them that there must be some mistake because she already had a licensor. They told her that her previous licensor had left the agency. Anne didn't understand why her licensor would leave the agency and not tell her. The supervisor informed Anne that they were visiting her to introduce her to her new licensor and to conduct an unannounced monitoring visit. Anne was so surprised that she didn't know what to say. Anne usually heard through the provider grapevine when her licensor was in town. Here were two strangers just dropping in on her at the worst possible time. As Anne began to explain this was not a good time, the supervisor abruptly asked if Anne was currently caring for children. When Anne replied she was, the supervisor informed her they were prepared to conduct a visit. (Reminder: In the majority of states, if you are open for child care, you cannot deny a licensor access to your program while actively caring for children.)

After Anne's visitors entered her kitchen, the woman who had introduced herself as Anne's new licensor immediately took out her laptop and started roaming around the first floor of Anne's home. The children, who sensed Anne's discomfort, started misbehaving as if on cue. As Anne was nervously attempting to calm the children, both licensors were walking throughout Anne's home whispering and typing furiously. (Reminder: Although licensors have the right to enter, you do have the right to request time to settle the children so that you can actively participate in the visit.)

When the visit concluded, Anne was left with two pages of citations, some of which were serious. The children who were present behaved badly throughout the visit, and Anne, who was so sure that she had been doing everything right, was left feeling discombobulated and incompetent. When Anne's assistant arrived, she found Anne at the kitchen table in tears, circled by a ring of confused children. How could this have happened? Anne had never had any issues with her licensing agency before, and now she and her business were in a mess!

DISCUSSION

This case study is based on actual events. Anne had total confidence in her relationship with her licensor. She relied on her licensor to keep her informed. Consequently, when Anne's licensor was no longer available, Anne was left in an extremely vulnerable position. As Anne reviewed the two pages of citations, she realized she had no idea whether the majority of her citations were valid or not. She sincerely did not understand how anything she had done that morning was out of compliance with her regulations. She had operated her program in the same manner for years—the only difference was that today two new licensors suddenly showed up at her door.

Anne began to realize that many of the things her previous licensor had told her about the operation of her program were said during visits when Anne was trying to do ten things at once. As a result, she hadn't been able to properly formulate questions or make sure she really understood. Anne also realized she had nothing in writing to prove how she had previously been instructed to operate her program. She felt angry and betrayed. When she attempted to explain all of this to the women conducting the visit, they did not appear to be interested. The supervisor explained that their role was to conduct a monitoring visit based on their observations at the time of their visit. They were not interested in previous visits made to Anne's program. The fact that Anne may have been unaware of some of the regulations was not their problem—it was Anne's.

The majority of Anne's citations were not serious. However, the cumulative effect of eighteen citations during a single monitoring visit was serious. In addition, the two citations identified as serious were of special concern. Anne attempted to explain that any violations included on the citation list were unintended. But her new licensor responded by telling Anne that her intentions, well-meaning or not, did not alter the seriousness of having the large number of citations.

Having two infants napping simultaneously in a playpen was determined to be a serious violation. Anne attempted to explain that she did not use the playpen for napping but did use it to keep the infants safe when she was alone and serving breakfast. She explained that she was unaware that she could not have the two infants sharing the same playpen. She really thought this was OK because the strategy of sharing the playpen was recommended by the twins' mother, who did this all the time at home. Anne was unaware that the regulations in her state prohibited infants from sleeping in a playpen in addition to prohibiting two children sharing the same napping equipment. Although Anne did not consider her playpen napping equipment, because the twins were sleeping in it when the licensors arrived, they believed they were required to issue a violation.

The second serious citation dealt with a knife left on the back of the kitchen counter. The knife was a butter knife that Anne had used to prepare breakfast. When Anne had run into the front room, she did so to grab a sweater she had left on the back of a chair. It was at that point she had seen the licensors through the window and directed them to her back door. Although she was out of the kitchen for only a few moments, both women saw her through the front window. Because Anne was seen in a room other than the kitchen, this became the rationale for citing Anne for leaving dangerous material accessible to children, in addition to a citation for inappropriate supervision.

Many of her citations were about clutter. Because she had not had the opportunity to clear her food prep area, the new licensor cited her for unsanitary conditions. This seemed especially unfair to Anne. She knew that she always kept a clean kitchen, and although she acknowledged that she hadn't had time to clear the remains of breakfast, that didn't mean her kitchen was unsanitary. Unfortunately, because Anne was unsure of the exact wording of her regulations, she did not feel confident enough to challenge the licensors' assessment.

Some of what occurred that morning—such as Anne's previous licensor leaving and having a new licensor conducting an unannounced monitoring visit accompanied by a supervisor—were beyond Anne's control. However, much of what did occur during Anne's visit could have been prevented. The following information contained in section 1 is designed to help you avoid Anne's predicament.

II. Regulations

Regulations define how your state requires you to operate your business. Regulations also define the consequences (that is, the types of legal action) a state may take against your license if it determines you are not operating according to the rules. As a small business owner who has made a significant investment of time and money, you need to understand your state's authority as it relates to your license. When and if a problem does occur, you don't want to be asking, "Can they really do that?" as you face sanctions or lose your license.

Your license is a legal document. Because of that, your licensing authority is required to follow specific legal procedures if they choose to act against your license. In most instances a licensing specialist cannot demand that you surrender your license at the time of your encounter. In most states the decision to revoke a license is not made at the time of the visit; the licensing agency must follow specific legal procedures. If the licensing authority chooses to take legal action against your license, they are required to inform you of your right to appeal.

READ THEM!

Although reading regulations may seem like an obvious thing to do, you might be surprised at the number of providers, like Anne, who don't read them. Please remember that despite any excuse, understanding your regulations is paramount to the success and protection of your business. Providers like Anne often assume there will always be someone available who has read the regulations and can tell them what they need to know. You could easily be jeopardizing your license if you make such an assumption. Using your licensor as a resource is recommended, but relying solely on someone else because you assume they know more about the appropriate operation of your business is never a good practice. This is especially true, as demonstrated in Anne's case, when that other person is unavailable when you need them.

No one is suggesting you read all your regulations in one sitting. However, you do need to read them—and, more importantly, you need to understand them. If you do not currently have a copy of your state's most recent regulations, get one! If your regulations are available only on your state's website, download them. During the operation of your business, always have a hard copy readily available to quickly refer to when needed. Often providers feel intimidated during a licensing visit. This is generally because many providers feel their licensor is better informed than they are. Surprisingly, that is not always the case. If you understand what's required of you, you are less likely to be taken advantage of. Too many providers, like Anne, only read their regulations once, when they are applying for a license. Familiarizing yourself with the language in your regulations is an ongoing responsibility. Don't jeopardize your business because you can't be bothered to understand the rules!

You don't have the luxury of only complying with regulations you agree with. If you have opinions about the practicality or the common sense of a regulation, the best time to voice your opinion is before a regulation is enacted. After the fact, you can certainly work to change or improve regulations, but while they exist in their current state, you have no choice but to comply. I have met providers like Anne who assumed that because they didn't understand, didn't agree, or weren't aware of a regulation, they could not be held responsible if they were found to be out of compliance. Generally, not understanding your regulations or complying with some regulations and not with others can have serious consequences. This is especially true if your regulatory violation can be connected to the injury or neglect of a child in your care.

UNDERSTAND THAT REGULATIONS ARE DIFFERENT FROM LAWS

Child care regulations are most frequently written with a focus on the protection of young children. Because of this, regulatory agencies usually have a great deal of leeway in how they develop requirements for licensure. Understand that regulations are not laws. Consequently, the legal rights that many people assume they have often don't apply in situations that require licensing intervention. For example, the assumption of "innocent until proven guilty" is not applicable in licensing investigations. As a result of an allegation, providers generally do not receive a presumption of innocence. The burden falls on you to demonstrate that you did not violate any regulations.

Regulations are frequently written in an open-ended fashion. This means they are usually open to interpretation and can be applied in a variety of ways. For example, most states have a regulation requiring early child care providers to "directly supervise" children. At first glance, the "direct supervision" regulation appears very straightforward. However, in family child care, where there is often only one caregiver, compliance with the supervision regulation can be complicated. Providers are human. Like everyone else, they occasionally need to use the bathroom. In addition, they are often responsible, as Anne was, for preparing meals, changing diapers, and attending to children who are upset or not feeling well. The reality of family child care doesn't always correspond with the open-ended language in most states' regulations. How you interpret and, in some instances, accommodate regulations can make a difference in whether you stay in business—or not. Anne made accommodations like the use of the playpen for the twins without determining whether that plan was appropriate. Many states have policy information available that interprets regulations by providing necessary details. Policy helps both providers and licensors understand how specific regulations should be applied in the daily operation of an early child care program. Reading and understanding your agency's policies is as important as reading and understanding regulations. Policy provides you with all the important details you need to protect your business.

NEVER ASSUME ANYTHING
Without the benefit of specific policies, providers often make assumptions. For example, in the case of "direct supervision," a provider may assume that when using the bathroom, keeping the bathroom door slightly ajar meets the intent of the supervision requirement. Another provider, reading the same regulation, might assume bringing all the children into the bathroom with her is the only way to accommodate this requirement. Unfortunately, depending on your state's supervision policy, one or both of these assumptions could be incorrect or incomplete. This may prove particularly relevant if a child is injured while

a provider is in the bathroom or if a parent issues a formal complaint about a child in the program accompanying an adult into the bathroom.

Anne made two assumptions. The first was based on the recommendation of a parent. She assumed it was okay to have two infants in one playpen, and that it was not a big issue if they fell asleep while waiting for her to finish with breakfast. The second assumption Anne made was that because she was leaving the kitchen for a few short moments, leaving the butter knife on the counter was not a problem. The truth is that you are a business owner, and you can't afford to guess. Anne guessed, and it resulted in problems. Having access to policy that defines specific regulations and understanding how to apply policy in the day-to-day operation of your program offers you some protection if something unintended occurs. Don't assume—ask questions and put the burden on your licensing agency to clarify specific regulations.

If you read your regulations, you will inevitably have questions. Frequently providers feel more comfortable asking questions of other providers, rather than asking a licensor. That's a mistake that can cost you. In Anne's case, she relied on advice from a parent, which turned out to be incorrect. If you receive inaccurate information from a friend and something unintended occurs as a result, it's all on you. If you receive inaccurate information from a licensor and something unintended occurs as a result, you have some protection. Both providers and licensors should understand that when a licensor offers direction or interpretation of a regulation, they are providing official regulatory policy.

When you ask for clarification from a licensor, document everything. Include the question, the answer, the name and contact information for the person you spoke to, and the date and time of your conversation. If you have the option of receiving your response in writing, via email or text, for example, it's to your benefit. If you are thinking about recording interactions with your licensor, make sure you understand the laws in your state. In many states you cannot record someone without their permission.

If you are confronted with a citation, saying, "My last licensor never told me that" or "No one I know does it that way," does not usually buy you any leeway. Unfortunately, Anne found this out the hard way. Regulatory agencies take issue with over-enrollment, inadequate adult/child ratio, inappropriate behavior management strategies, an unsanitary environment, inadequate supervision, and similar infractions. This means before you make any program changes or big decisions that can affect your business, be sure to reread all relevant regulations and policies. Ask questions when necessary. Make sure any current program decisions you make won't jeopardize your future ability to operate a successful business. For example, if you are building a deck and you intend to use it for child care, double-check all the necessary regulatory requirements. Keep in mind that regulatory requirements and building permit requirements are not always the same. Don't place yourself in a situation where you build a deck and then find out you can't use it for child care.

If a licensing issue does occur, your best protection is reliable documentation, full knowledge of regulations and policies, and an accurate understanding of your rights as a licensed provider.

III. POLICY

Being able to demonstrate compliance with regulations using program-specific policy helps if you have to defend your business from false or inaccurate allegations. A good way to demonstrate your compliance is to be able to produce the specific instruction or policy you used to support your decisions. One good strategy for retrieving this type of information is to create a personalized Policy Manual.

Whatever occurs in your program is ultimately your responsibility. Maintaining a manual with current and accurate information can go a long way to help you protect your business now and in the future.

It's smart to create a manual specific to your program because every child care facility and every facility operator is different. Frequently, situations that are uncommon or even unique to your environment require program-specific clarification. For example, Anne was caring for twin infants. If Anne had been aware of her state's policy clarifying the restrictions on using playpens, she would have chosen a different method to accommodate the twins.

Many of you have already begun collecting information during monitoring visits or state-sponsored training without necessarily identifying it as policy. Often this type of material gets discarded or stored away someplace where you can't find it. I have heard providers who find themselves in trouble say they initially made a program decision "based on something they heard or read." Unfortunately, when challenged, like Anne, they had nothing in writing to back them up. Having an organized manual that allows you to retrieve relevant information when you need it goes a long way to professionalize and protect your business.

Having a personalized Policy Manual helps you avoid the assumption that a licensor, a parent, or anyone else who has a different interpretation of a regulation is automatically right, and you are wrong. For example, often providers complain that when a new licensor is assigned to their program, all of a sudden the rules change. Keeping documentation readily available that shows how you've been previously instructed provides you with important evidence and some protection.

CREATING A POLICY BINDER

A good way to begin your policy binder is to obtain a two-inch, three-ring binder. Using this type of binder allows you to review your policy information periodically and discard any information that's outdated or inaccurate.

- Find out where and how to obtain your state's early child care policy information. Some states keep policy and regulatory information in one location on their website. However, in other states, policy may be dispersed randomly. Save yourself valuable time by asking what the practice is in your state. Your licensor should be able to tell you where to locate policy information or at least send you in the right direction. On occasion policy may be available to licensors but not providers. In those instances, creating your own manual becomes increasingly important so you can refer to policy in your binder.
- Review copies of all visit reports resulting from licensing or monitoring visits. If you are not currently receiving copies of visit reports, request them. If the practice in your state requires that you go online to review data collected during a monitoring visit, ask questions: What is the procedure for correcting inaccurate information that appears online? What can you do if online information contains citations that were not

discussed at the time of the visit? Are you able to add clarification to what appears on your licensing portal? Include any clarification you receive in your policy binder. Any technical assistance or comments that clarify regulations or provide specific program direction should also be placed in your binder. When you receive new information (during a licensing visit, for example), check to see whether it corresponds with your existing policy information. If there are inconsistencies, tell your licensor. If you are told a policy has changed, request a copy of the new policy. If a licensor is unable to explain why their interpretation does not correspond with the policy information you currently possess, document their explanation and request written clarification and, if necessary, a second opinion.

- As you collect policy information, it's easier to organize your binder by dividing it into sections. Create individual sections by labeling dividers with corresponding regulations. Some examples include Supervision, Quota and Adult/Child Ratio, Behavior Management, Health and Safety, Physical Environment, and Safe Sleep Requirements. Whatever way you decide to organize your binder, keep in mind that you are not simply filing things away. You want a binder that works for you and allows you to quickly find specific information whenever you need it.

- You may find that you collect policy information in a variety of ways. A licensor or another professional may share printed resource material. When possible, ask to have the material signed and dated. Often you may receive policy information verbally. It is smart to request an email or text confirming what you've been told. If that is not possible, document what was said and, whenever possible, have the individual sign and date your documentation.

- Occasionally providers share their personal interpretation of a specific regulation with one another. If something sounds too good to be true, it probably is. Before you introduce any policy information you get from a friend or client family, make sure you contact your licensing agency and ask questions. You can simply share what you've heard and ask if the information is accurate. If the information is validated, you can include it in your policy binder, with the name and date of the person you spoke with. If you are told the information is inaccurate, you may want to tell your friend.

- Although you may or may not look forward to monitoring visits, those visits provide an opportunity for you to collect important information. Don't be shy about asking questions. It's a good idea to keep a running list of questions that come up during the normal operation of your business.

- At the conclusion of a site visit, you are usually required to sign something before your licensor leaves your program. Always give yourself the opportunity to read before signing. Keep in mind that you are not obliged to sign anything that contains inaccurate or false information. However, if you choose not to sign, make sure you are prepared to demonstrate why you believe the information contained in the report is false. Remember, you should always request a copy of any documentation compiled during a program visit. If it is not available to you at the time of visit, make sure you understand where and how to retrieve that information. Reading and then highlighting comments that include specific direction, correction, or clarification will give you additional information for your binder. I strongly recommend you use your own Monitoring Visit Log during a visit. This has become increasingly important for providers who live in states where you do not receive a copy of your licensor's visit log at the conclusion of a visit. Using a Monitoring Visit Log allows you an organized way to collect information as well as to reinforce shared accountability with the professionals who visit your program.

MONITORING VISIT LOG

Using your own organized format to collect information during a professional visit can save you time and trouble. When creating a Monitoring Visit Log, make sure you do the following:

- Always record the date and time of a visit. Document your licensor's time in and time out during the visit. This information becomes useful if you need to prove that the number and duration of visits made to your program appear excessive. Remember that in most states, if you are open and caring for children, you cannot deny access to a licensing representative. You may be in your own home; however, you are operating a business in your home, and your business is subject to regulatory oversight. If you believe you are being treated unfairly, you can use your Monitoring Logs as a way to validate your observations.

- Ask the purpose of an unannounced visit. You have the right to know the reason for an official visit to your program (monitoring, renewal, investigation, and so on). Make sure you write down names, titles, accurate contact information, and the expressed reason for a program visit.
- Document any positive comments you receive during a visit. Positive feedback can be important if you are appealing an agency decision. Unfortunately, positive comments are rarely included in agency documentation. It's up to you to make sure you have a record of all the good things said about your program. If, by the end of the visit, you have not received any positive comments, don't be shy about asking the visitor for any positive observations they can share.
- If you are cited, make sure you receive specific information about the regulation or policy used to justify the citation. If your licensor is unable to identify a specific regulation, have your regulations available so that you and your licensor can review the regulatory language together. This information, along with any recommended corrections, is especially important if you choose to challenge a citation.
- Respectfully request a signature and date for your documentation. If the professional visiting your program refuses to sign, document their refusal.
- Realize that visit logs are a snapshot of your program and reflect a moment in time. Use your documentation to provide context to ensure that the licensor's snapshot is an accurate overall portrayal of you and your business.

THE COMMENT SECTION

When I worked as a licensor, it was a common practice to include a comment section in a provider's licensing file. This was a place for a licensor to record observations or impressions that would not be included on the licensor's visit log. These comments were generally included back at the office after a visit had been concluded. Consequently, providers did not have access to the notes contained in the comment section. In some instances, this information was a heads-up for the licensor or their successor for any subsequent monitoring visits.

The information was not always criticism—there were certainly occasions when licensors included positive comments regarding the program or the provider. Often the comments included a reminder for a licensor to follow up on potential issues they observed at the time of the visit. Some comments were personal in nature, such as the death of a provider's family member, the birth of a new child, or other information that might flag a provider as a candidate for additional support.

I recommend that providers create their own comment section as an addendum to their Monitoring Visit Log. Do not include it with the information contained in your Monitoring Visit Log unless you choose to share your personal observations with the individual signing your log. As noted earlier, there are times when a provider is unsure whether a licensor has crossed the line in terms of conduct or attitude. It is difficult to make a case without having anything to back you up. Adding a comment section allows you to create organized documentation about any concerns, impressions, or additional questions you may have. Try to make your comments as soon after the visit as possible. You want to make sure that you are accurately representing what was said and what occurred during the visit. You can download the sample Monitoring Visit Log by scanning this QR code or visiting www.redleafpress.org/pyb/1-1.pdf.

SAMPLE MONITORING VISIT LOG

DATE: _____   TIME IN: _____   TIME OUT: _____

NAME(S) OF VISITOR(S): _____

_____

PROFESSIONAL TITLE: _____

AGENCY/ORGANIZATION: _____

CONTACT INFORMATION: (OFFICE) _____ (CELL) _____

(E-MAIL) _____

PURPOSE OF VISIT: _____

POSITIVE FEEDBACK: _____

_____

CITED NONCOMPLIANCE(S):

REGULATION AND/OR POLICY # _____

CITATION: _____

_____

RECOMMENDED CORRECTION: _____

_____

_____

ADDITIONAL QUESTIONS AND/OR COMMENTS: _____

_____

_____

HOME VISITOR'S SIGNATURE AND DATE:

_____

IV. Preventing Common Citations

For some of you, the information contained in this section may appear redundant. I have included it because citations regarding health and safety, along with supervision, make up the largest percentage of citations received by providers. These are avoidable citations regardless of whether a visit is announced or a licensor shows up when you least expect it. Remember that regulations exist to keep children safe, and often new regulations are added because children have suffered injuries. Using checklists, paying attention to your environment, and staying current with requirements are all great ways to keep your business citation-free!

THE DAILY FABRIC OF YOUR PROGRAM

I have seen creative and child-friendly environments in thousands of family child care programs, and there are many resources available to help you create an appropriate early child care environment in your home without turning your entire house into a child care center. Your arrangement of space and materials should be in keeping with both your physical environment and your preference for how you want to structure your program. It's great to examine a variety of positive examples, but because every home, family, and provider is unique, it's important that you create an environment that accurately reflects your personal and professional goals. It is much easier to maintain regulatory compliance when you and the other individuals who live in your household feel comfortable and confident about your environment.

It's a good idea to create a daily checklist you can use before opening your door to receive children. Inevitably, the day you don't check is the day you receive an unannounced visit from your licensor. It's just good practice to start each day knowing something easily corrected is not going to cause unnecessary problems. Things such as reinserting outlet covers and quickly cleaning counters and floors are an easy fix. What do you smell? Are there any pet odors, or is there garbage that needs to go out? Have you checked yourself in the mirror? What are families and children seeing as they walk through your door? Don't jeopardize your business with unnecessary citations.

The following are five major areas to check daily:

1. Entrance—the first impression
2. General Health and Safety—how your program demonstrates your focus on the health and safety of participating children
3. Caregiving Areas—where eating, sleeping, diapering, and practicing good hygiene take place
4. Learning Environment—how your environment facilitates growth and development
5. Outdoor Play Space—where children experience nature and can engage in activities that promote good physical health

Entrance

Usually the first impression families and visitors have of your business is the entry. Make sure the first impression is as positive as possible—a violation seen as soon as the licensor arrives at your program can set the tone for the entire licensing visit. If your program is located in a multifamily dwelling or in a shared commercial space, you may not have a great deal of control over your entry. However, you should continue to look for ways to present a safe and welcoming appearance. If you are renting, familiarize your landlord or building manager with your obligation to provide a safe environment in common areas used by children. This becomes especially important when trash storage or disposal occurs near the entrance to your child care facility. In some instances, providers find themselves in trouble for issues they consider to be beyond their control. In most states your licensed environment includes your entry and any other common areas accessible to children. You will, in most cases, be held responsible for the appropriateness of common areas.

Many states implemented new requirements during the COVID-19 pandemic that affected how clients and children enter your facility. Some providers welcomed these changes and have incorporated them into the ongoing operation of their programs. For example, you may want to establish one designated entry. A designated entry might include space to post instructions for parents/guardians. Each parent or guardian may be required to attest to the health of children by initialing a sign-in sheet. Every provider knows that communicable diseases such as colds and strep throat are common problems in most early child care environments. Introducing requirements that minimize contagion helps to protect not only enrolled children but also you, your staff, and your household members. Many providers have used this method to reinforce their program's sick policy.

It's to your advantage when the entry to your program is maintained appropriately. Here are some suggestions to ensure that you put your best foot forward when entering your child care program:

- Keep floors clean and protected from dirt and moisture.
- Illuminate the entry space with proper lighting.
- Ensure that there are no tripping hazards.
- If your entry has stairs, make sure they are appropriately gated when required.
- Have the necessary measures in place to ensure that unwanted visitors do not enter the child care premises.
- Install a device or method to alert you if an unaccompanied child leaves the premises.
- When possible, maintain separate storage space for each child's personal belongings.

General Health and Safety

Health and safety issues continue to be important. Read any new requirements carefully. (See pages 23–30 for specific health and safety information.) Use this list to help ensure that your child care environment follows general health and safety requirements:

- The space smells clean and fresh. Make sure there are no odors from improper diaper disposal, smoking, garbage, pets, air fresheners, or harsh or strong-smelling disinfectants.
- You and any other staff understand and comply with any requirements regarding daily hand washing.
- The room temperature is controllable and set at a comfortable level.
- Ventilation is appropriate in all spaces used by children.
- Furniture and equipment are safe and sturdy and periodically checked for any product safety recalls.
- Lighting is sufficient in areas used by children.

- Radiators, fans, and air conditioners are securely installed with appropriate barriers.
- Low windows above the first floor have child-safe barriers.
- The facility is certified lead safe, when applicable.
- Hazardous materials and objects are stored in locked spaces out of reach of children. Review your regulations to ensure that you understand which common items are considered hazardous.
- Electrical outlets are covered.
- Window blinds don't have hanging cords.
- A first aid kit is available in the child care space.
- Fire safety measures are in place in accordance with your regulations.
- A sick area is designated where you can separate a sick child from the larger child care group but still be in in your line of vision until the child can safely leave the program.

Caregiving Areas

Caregiving areas are the locations where children's physical needs are met, including diapering and toileting, naps and rest, meals, and the teaching of good hygiene practices such as brushing teeth and washing hands.

- Children have a designated eating area, which includes high chairs with appropriate restraints.
- The food prep area is safe and clean and, when possible, arranged to allow for children's participation.
- Each child has their own cot, mat, or bed that meets licensing codes (as well as safe sleep requirements).
- Cribs meet Consumer Product Safety Commission (CPSC) safety standards (regularly check reliable recall information at www.cpsc .gov/Recalls).
- The light level can be reduced for sleep, but the room is not completely dark.
- An area is available for nonnapping children to read and play quietly.
- Space is available for infants to sleep as needed on their own schedule.
- The space is arranged so that children can be easily supervised when sleeping.

- The diapering area is safe and hygienic and situated so the provider can see and/or hear other children at all times.
- Diapering is not done near the food prep area or any sink used for food prep.
- The diapering surface is easily cleaned and sanitized.
- The bathroom used by children is clean, safe, and appropriate.
- If potty chairs or child-sized toilet seats are used, they are sanitized after each use.
- Materials to sanitize hands and surfaces as required are available.

Learning Environment

In early child care, every aspect of your environment should provide young children with the opportunity to develop a variety of skills. It is not necessary to try to replicate large centers or institutions like public schools to facilitate skill development. Your knowledge about how to facilitate healthy growth and development in young children is one of your most important superpowers! Look for resources that will help you introduce a productive but doable daily routine. Think about how to store and recycle materials for each activity. Avoid the appearance of clutter as much as possible. Many resources are available with great recommendations on how to create appropriate, home-friendly learning environments. Choose resources specifically designed to support home-based child care. Don't be afraid to ask for help.

- Whenever possible it's helpful (but not necessary) to have separate zones for active, quiet, and messy play. If this is not realistic for you, think about which areas of your home can do double duty so that various areas can be used for a variety of activities rather than only one type of activity.
- Areas can be defined by using furniture arrangements, rugs, or room dividers. You can also use child care materials and equipment such as child-sized tables and chairs or a bookcase to define the intended use of a space. It's also exciting to see how children perceive a space and the types of activities they introduce.
- Your entire environment needs to be arranged for the easy supervision of children. This is a constant refrain throughout this guide as

allegations of inappropriate supervision are extremely common in early child care.

- Both adults and children can easily move around the space.
- A range of age-appropriate materials are available to children.
- Items are labeled with words and pictures (when appropriate).
- Learning materials are sturdy and safe.
- Your environment has an appropriate area for creating art, including easy access to water and art supplies.
- Electronic equipment is used appropriately in the environment, and no electronic equipment is accessible to children under the age of two.
- An accessible book area offers a variety of age-appropriate books.
- Soft surfaces and cozy areas are available.
- Your environment includes comfortable adult seating for holding or rocking infants.

When examining your environment, you may decide to move around some materials or equipment or put some into storage to maximize usable space.

Outdoor Play Space

Moving your program outdoors as the weather permits can help promote the healthy well-being of participating children. Additionally, in most states daily outdoor play is required. Outdoor activity can be a great way to broaden the types of activities you make available to children. Frequently, providers may find organizing a group of multiaged children to go outside, especially in cold weather, a challenging task. If children are dressed appropriately, they should be able to go outside during winter months. Organize your program in a way that helps you get children outdoors and helps you avoid unnecessary citations. For example, I have encountered providers who encourage families of children in their program to volunteer to help organize and participate in outdoor activities. To provide a safe outdoor space, ensure the following:

- Your outside space complies with regulations regarding fences or natural barriers.
- There are no hazards such as broken glass, animal waste, nails, poisonous plants, standing water, and so on.

- Trash cans are secured and inaccessible to children.
- Lawn mowers and other tools are stored securely.
- A first aid kit and phone are easily accessible.
- The yard or alternative outdoor play space has clear sightlines and no hidden areas to hinder supervision.
- The outdoor play space has areas with both sun and shade.
- Play equipment is safe, sturdy, and in good repair.
- Play equipment is age appropriate.

If you are using an alternative outdoor play space, such as a park or school yard, you have an obligation to make sure that the environment you use is suitable and safe for children. Your responsibility does not end at your front door.

PREVENTING INJURIES AND HEALTH AND SAFETY ISSUES

According to statistics from the Centers for Disease Control and Prevention, injuries are the number one killer of children in the United States. While rare, injuries and deaths do occur in child care. Because of this, be as proactive as possible when examining your environment. Regulatory agencies usually focus on compliance with all regulations at the time of the incident, despite the recognition that accidents do occur. You may not be personally responsible for an accident, but if there was a regulatory issue when the accident occurred, your program may be jeopardized. Believing unintentional incidents can happen only in other programs can endanger children in your program and make you and your business vulnerable.

Falls

Most children are eager to walk, run, climb, or move to the maximum of their ability. Introducing safety gates and creating fall-safe environments (carpeting, blankets, pillows, and so on) are ways to minimize injury. Most young children fall frequently as they are learning to stand and walk, so create environments that acknowledge how young children develop while continuing to keep them safe. Your role as an early child care provider includes the facilitation of children's healthy growth and development. Restraining young children in a manner that impedes their development is not a legitimate safety plan.

Poisoning

Young children usually want to touch, taste, and smell all the things around them. That's why it's so important to maintain a hazard-free environment. Don't make assumptions about the toxicity of products without carefully examining labels. This is also true for pet foods and products labeled organic or natural. Make sure you read labels with a special emphasis on warnings about ingredients that may be damaging to children. Providers are usually diligent about keeping medicines and items such as bleach inaccessible. However, providers use a variety of methods to sanitize their environments. While you may wish to keep sprays, wipes, and sanitizers handy because you are using them frequently, they must remain secure from children at all times.

Choking

Learn about potential choking hazards so you can avoid an incident. Make sure when families are sending food from home or are requesting that you provide certain types of food (such as allowing very young children to eat finger foods such as fruits and raw vegetables earlier than is traditionally recommended) that you are getting second opinions if you feel a child is not ready or you are unsure of regulatory requirements. Ask questions.

Drowning

Not every family child care provider uses a swimming pool during the operation of their program. For those of you who do, you have a special obligation to make sure every child is supervised and supported in a manner that protects them from drowning. I would recommend consulting with an attorney before using your pool during child care. It's wise to discuss potential liability issues and to seek help in developing appropriate and comprehensive permission forms. A supervision policy that addresses water play can be extremely important. Any distraction, even a momentary one, can be disastrous. Understand your regulatory requirements regarding the use of a pool.

For those of you who do not use a pool, still remember that young children can drown in a very small amount of water. There should never be an occasion when a young child is near standing water without supervision, regardless of depth. Always organize your program in a way that makes direct supervision and immediate access to every child as easy as possible.

Fire/Burns

Obviously, children need to be kept away from hot ovens and open flames. However, outdoor equipment placed in the sun, as well as lamps or lighting with accessible bulbs can also cause burns. Be diligent in keeping your child care environment hazard-free. Allow for required review of smoke and carbon monoxide detectors. Conduct practice evacuations as required.

Unexpected Incidents

I was the licensor on call when a tree limb unexpectedly fell from a tree and instantly killed a three-year-old child who was riding his Big Wheel in his provider's driveway. Meeting with this child's parents and seeing the devastation his death caused for everyone involved was something I will never forget. We are all busy, and when things are going well it's sometimes easy to become complacent. You have chosen a profession that does not allow you that luxury. Unfortunately, some incidents cannot be avoided. Things beyond your control sometimes happen regardless of how well you operate your program. It's in those instances that your ability to demonstrate that you were following all regulations at the time of the incident helps protect your business.

Hygiene and Sanitation

The year I opened my child care, I bought a lot of tissues and took a lot of aspirin. I had headaches, flu-like symptoms, and a constant runny nose, and I almost always felt I was either coming down with or in the middle of a head cold. When I questioned my doctor and he found out what I did for a living, he laughed and said I should get used to it. I quickly learned it was a running joke that early child care environments are a breeding ground for communicable diseases.

Later when I worked as a licensor, I found it was not uncommon to enter an early child care facility and find everyone in the group, including the provider, sharing the same cold. Providers frequently complained about parents/guardians who would ignore the program's sick policy and drop off children who were both contagious and sick. I would bet almost every provider has had experience with a child who was given acetaminophen before coming to child care, only to be symptomatic by noon. I have heard that same story a thousand times.

Recently, however, I've heard providers say that they are seeing a decrease in the number of common colds and other common communicable diseases in their programs. Many providers believe the new sanitation routines introduced as a result of COVID-19 have helped to keep programs healthier than ever before.

Here are some tips to slow the spread of illness:

- Use liquid soap. Bars of soap may collect germs from the previous user, which can spread when others use the soap. Most children seem to like liquid soap, which makes them more likely to use it every time they wash their hands.
- Use warm running water. Cold water is less effective at removing germs than warm water. But remember that young children can be burned by water that is too hot. To prevent burns, be sure your hot water supply does not get hotter than 120 degrees Fahrenheit.
- Scrub hands for at least twenty seconds. The process of scrubbing hands together helps remove grime and germs. Teach children to sing a hand-washing song while they wash their hands to help them remember to scrub thoroughly. Singing a song like "Twinkle, Twinkle, Little Star" or "Happy Birthday" through twice should take about twenty seconds.
- Use disposable single-use towels. A shared hand towel in the bathroom is a prime spot for germs to grow and spread. Disposable paper towels and tissues go a long way toward preventing illness by reducing the opportunity to share germs. Reinforce appropriate disposal of paper towels.
- Use hand sanitizers sparingly. Routine hand washing should happen with liquid soap and warm running water. Hand sanitizers may be better than nothing when soap and water are not available (such as on field trips) but should never replace hand washing with soap and water. Hand sanitizers contain ethanol, which is toxic if ingested, and are not a safe option for children under two who may put their hands in their mouths. Baby wipes can be used to wipe infants' and toddlers' hands when there is no soap and water. Keep all hand sanitizers out of the reach of children.

- Wash infants' and toddlers' hands too. Some child care providers forget to wash infants' and toddlers' hands with running water because it's difficult to get them in the right position at a sink. Proper hand washing begins in infancy, and washing infants' and toddlers' hands is an important way to teach them proper hand washing and prevent the spread of germs. As infants and toddlers grow, encourage them to begin washing their hands independently. A step stool may come in handy to help raise children to sink level, but make sure you never leave young children unattended around water.
- Follow standard procedures for cleaning as recommended by the Environmental Protection Agency (EPA). Typically, this means daily sanitizing of surfaces and objects that are frequently touched, such as bathrooms, water dispensers, desks, tables, countertops, doorknobs, computer keyboards, hands-on learning items, faucet handles, phones, and toys.
- Make disinfecting your responsibility or the responsibility of your staff. Obtain training so you use disinfectants in a safe and effective manner to clean up potentially infectious materials and body fluid spills—blood, vomit, feces, and urine. Clean the surface first to remove all organic matter. Follow the disinfectant manufacturer's instructions for use:

  - Use the proper concentration of disinfectant.
  - Allow the required wet contact time.
  - Pay close attention to hazard warnings and instructions for using personal protective items such as gloves and eye protection.
  - Use disinfectants in a sufficiently ventilated space.

- Look into storing materials and toys for each child in separate storage containers or baskets, which helps minimize shared exposure. If you used this procedure in your program during the COVID-19 pandemic, think about continuing to implement some form of this practice.
- Think about continuing (or implementing) daily health screening routines. This usually includes parents/guardians attesting to the health of their children. Some providers have continued to do temperature checks

after COVID-19. Find ways that work for both you and your child care families to contribute to a healthy environment.

- Consider your environment. We have always known children need space to play and grow, but many of you have recently made changes to your environment to facilitate social distancing. Many providers have moved or stored large equipment or furniture that takes up lots of valuable space. Providers have shared suggestions like using small portable tables for children to use for eating and doing projects that can be sanitized and folded away after each use. A lot of providers have found new and creative ways to meet the developmental needs of children in care without large pieces of equipment. The benefits of freeing up space include improving your ability to more easily supervise children, allowing more open space for activities, and making cleanup easier. Consider which changes you've made to your environment that have had good results. Think about including them in the future.

Pets

Thoroughly investigate the appropriateness of any animal you choose to introduce to young children. If you are unsure about the safe and healthy inclusion of pets, refer to your regulations and your local health department. For example, pets such as lizards, turtles, parrots, and ferrets can create health problems and are not recommended in early child care settings. Cat and rabbit fur can be the source of allergic reactions, and exposure to substances such as kitty litter is not safe for young children.

Consider including questions at the time of enrollment regarding any pet-specific allergies. When thinking about adding pets, it can also be helpful to understand each child's past experiences with animals that may have been traumatic or uncomfortable. Use a Family Survey (see p. 46) to periodically determine each family's comfort level with your inclusion of pets. Family child care providers have a special responsibility to ensure that a beloved household pet is not victimized unintentionally by young children. As a small business owner, it's to your advantage to minimize your liability while protecting children. In family child care, keep in mind that while it is your home, it's also your place of business. Having a separate place for family pets during child care hours can help you avoid potential problems.

Food Allergies

Since January 2006 federal law has required all major allergens to be clearly listed on labels. Know what you're purchasing. If a family has identified an enrolled child's food allergy, do not purchase food products that contain that substance, even if you have served that same food to children in the past with no negative consequences. Once you've received information about an enrolled child's food allergy, you invite potential liability if you do not take all precautions necessary to keep that child safe.

If families are unaware of a food allergy and you notice that a child develops symptoms after being exposed to certain foods while in your care, notify the child's family at once. Symptoms can include but are not limited to hives, rashes, swollen tongue and lips, or difficulty breathing. Depending on the severity of symptoms, follow your emergency procedures immediately. When the child returns to child care, start a diary in collaboration with the child's family to record which foods the child has been eating, especially anything newly introduced.

Sudden Infant Death Syndrome (SIDS)

Most states currently require providers to take safe sleep training. Find out whether this is a requirement in your state. If it's not, consider taking a safe sleep workshop anyway. It contains lifesaving information that every provider should be aware of. Once you've taken this training, use what you learn in the daily operation of your business.

Create a safe sleep policy for your program and share it with your child care families. Make sure anyone working in your program is familiar with approved safe sleep practices. The following are some examples of what you may include in your policy:

- Manage your program so that an approved adult is available to supervise napping infants at all times. (Most states require sleeping infants to be supervised at all times.)
- Position ALL infants on their backs when sleeping.

- Reposition sleeping infants on their backs until they can roll over independently.
- Don't allow napping infants to sleep with stuffed animals, pillows, or quilts.
- Use well-maintained napping equipment. Check periodically for recalled equipment. Ensure that crib mattresses fit appropriately and there are no gaps between the mattress and crib frame.

For some reason, some providers believe that if a parent/guardian requests that "baby sleep with a favorite blanket or toy" or says that "baby sleeps better on his stomach," it is OK to be flexible. It's not. A parental/guardian preference does not supersede your obligation to adhere to safe sleep regulations. I represented a provider who followed a parent's direction, although the direction was in contrast to what the provider knew was required by regulation. The infant was injured while napping. The parent's response when made aware of this incident was to tell the provider, "You should have known better; you're supposed to be the professional."

Frankly, you're not required to agree with all regulations, only to comply. That may sound harsh, but in this example, if the provider had followed safe sleep requirements at the time this child was injured, she most probably would have been OK. She didn't follow regulations because she thought she was making the parent happy by allowing a toy in the crib and assumed the parent's wishes superseded her regulations. As a result, the provider's license was jeopardized.

SUPERVISION REQUIREMENTS

Because inadequate supervision is one of the leading causes of citations and complaints, examining your supervision policy is a good place to begin. For some of you this might sound like unnecessary and additional work. But those of you who have experienced licensing intervention likely have learned that taking proactive steps before something occurs could have saved you headaches and a lot of stress. Licensors are not only responsible for helping you understand regulations but also for providing instruction about how to appropriately comply with regulations. Too often providers guess. That is not a realistic practice if you want to continue to operate a successful business.

When setting up your environment, your ability to easily supervise is a priority. When activities are grouped together and furniture is waist high or lower, adults should be able to see and/or hear children. Child care areas should be kept clutter free and set up so that children have clear play spaces that allow adults an unobstructed view. The following are some key things to know about providing proper supervision.

Arrange Your Space for Supervision and Functionality

Your first priority in setting up your environment should be ease of supervision. When providing family child care, think carefully about the rooms you choose to use. You need to think about what organization of space and activities will make supervision as easy as possible. Asking "How can I ensure safety when I have to use the bathroom, make lunch, or change a diaper?" is important when considering how to organize your space. The arrangement of your space should reflect the developmental stages of the children enrolled in your program. If your enrollment is made up primarily of infants and young toddlers, your environment should be arranged to facilitate the children who are in that stage of development. Do not feel it's necessary to create a preschool space when you do not currently have preschoolers enrolled in your program. In family child care it is especially important to use space wisely. Think about the function, purpose, and ease of supervision before arranging your space.

Understand Policies Clarifying Supervision Requirements

As discussed, most states have policies that clarify supervision regulations. You need to understand all regulations and policies dealing with supervision. Regulatory agencies focus on compliance. If a child is injured as a result of an incident while in child care, your regulatory agency will perform an investigation to determine whether your program was following all regulations at the time of the incident. If there is a question regarding your intent at the time of the incident, generally a social service agency will join the investigation and decide the question of possible abuse or neglect. Regulatory agencies determine whether all regulations were adhered to at the time an incident occurred. Social service agencies most frequently determine intent.

In some cases, providers may be required to "see and/or hear children." Provisions may also allow providers and/or staff to supervise from adjacent rooms. In some instances, there may be a specific distance/time ratio that specifies how quickly you need to be able to intercede if you or your staff are in adjacent space. Frequently there are specific supervision requirements for different age groups. It's important to note that you should not introduce any new supervision policy or practice that is different from what is in your regulations without first obtaining approval from your licensing agency. Don't take on that liability. Your state's licensing agency has a responsibility to identify what constitutes appropriate supervision in a licensed child care facility. Don't assume their responsibility—you already have enough of your own.

Position Yourself and/or Your Staff

You need to position yourself and/or your staff in a way that protects children from harm. Make sure there are always clear paths to where children are playing, sleeping, and eating so you can react quickly when necessary. Stay close to children who may need additional supervision.

Scan and Count

You need to be able to account for all the children in your care. Continually scan the entire environment to know where everyone is and what they're doing. Count heads frequently. Pay special attention during transitions when children are moving from one location to another. Children leaving child care programs without being noticed is not as unusual as it should be. Providers and staff on cell phones, inappropriate adult/child ratio, or any distraction that takes adult focus away from participating children can be a recipe for trouble. Unintended incidents can occur in any program at any time. If a child does leave your program without permission, the amount of time the child is gone before you discover the absence will have a huge bearing on any subsequent investigation. The burden falls on you, if something should occur, to demonstrate that your program complied with all supervision requirements. If you have had a previous licensing intervention due to a supervision issue, you do not want to have a second intervention for the same reason. Your second intervention could very well end your ability to maintain your license.

Anticipate Children's Behavior

Most providers do not operate with crystal balls, but knowing each child's temperament, interests, and skills often allows you to predict what they might do next. This is a real advantage in family child care, where you have a unique opportunity to get to know each child well. It can be a persuasive talking point when interviewing potential clients. It's appropriate to create challenges and try new things (a trip to the park, for example), but you also need to choose activities that correspond with the abilities of all the children in your group. You need to be aware of children who are apt to wander, get upset, or take dangerous risks. Providers who know what to expect are better able to protect children from harm and avoid incidents and complaints. Determining what was a "foreseeable occurrence" can often play a large role in any agency investigation.

Listen

As most providers know, specific sounds—or the absence of them—often signify reasons for concern. Providers and staff who listen closely to children can often immediately identify signs of potential danger. Providers who think proactively implement additional safeguards. For example, bells attached to doors are a simple and inexpensive way to alert you when someone is leaving or entering the program. More sophisticated alarm systems are also available.

Have Plans in Place When Working Alone

If you work alone, you should have a plan in place for how you will protect all the children when you are using the bathroom, preparing food, changing a diaper, and so forth. Sometimes a provider has a plan in place but then forgets about it. Time passes, enrollment changes, and it's easy to become complacent. Your plan should correspond with the ages and developmental stages of children currently in your care. This means that as your enrollment changes, so should your supervision plan. Sharing your supervision plan with your child care families can help to prevent issues. Anyone working with you should also acknowledge their understanding with their signature. It's also a good idea to have your supervision plan reviewed by your licensor. If something unintended should occur, the fact that a licensor reviewed and approved your plan will provide you with some protection. I recently consulted with a provider who quite literally saved her license because she had a camera system installed on her front and back door. An allegation was made, the provider was able to demonstrate with a copy of her recordings what actually occurred, and the provider was immediately vindicated.

Formulate a Plan for Children Arriving and Leaving by Bus

Some children are transported to and from a family child care program by bus or van. It's not uncommon for providers to be told "it's their responsibility" to accompany children to and from the bus. If you have assistants working in your program during the hours when children are transported, this may not be a problem. However, many family child care providers do not employ staff or do not have staff available at the time of transport. Please keep in mind that anyone left alone with child care children should have appropriate approval.

If you are usually working alone during these periods and you have agreed to be responsible for children leaving or entering a bus, create a formal plan. In creating a supervision plan, be realistic. If your plan includes bringing all the children who are present outside with you, keep in mind the reality of the weather and the ages of children in your program. Bringing every child out to the bus may not be a realistic plan. Never assume that because you "only ran outside for a moment" you can't be held responsible if a child left inside gets injured. Whatever plan you create, make sure it's a plan you can realistically employ. Have your plan reviewed by your licensor to help ensure that you have some protection if something unintended occurs.

Discuss this issue with the company responsible for transporting children. If a sufficient number of concerned stakeholders identify this as an issue, companies may employ bus monitors who can supervise young children going to and from the bus. Talk with other providers and enlist the aid of your child care families. Find out what options are available. Be proactive and advocate for accommodations that keep children safe and offer realistic options for you.

TRAVEL AND TRANSPORTATION ISSUES

Many providers take their program on the road, especially during seasons of good weather. Every day is a different field trip: library, park, children's museum, beach, and so forth.

If you are using your car to transport children in your program, always use appropriate child safety/booster seats and ensure that they are installed and fastened properly. Make sure you understand not only your licensing regulations (required permission forms, child care records, safety equipment, and so on) but also the laws in your state regarding the transport of child care children. Providers have sometimes assumed that if they are complying with licensing regulations they are protected. Many states have strict requirements regarding the transport of children that are unrelated to licensing regulations. For example, if you are transporting children as part of your program's daily routine, some states require a special category of license and/or registration. Many states also have additional insurance requirements when transporting children as part of your business. Contact your local Registry of Motor Vehicles or Department of Motor Vehicles to obtain accurate information. Ignoring a requirement because it may involve additional expense is not worth it. It is better not to transport at all if you feel your state requirements create too much of a financial burden or other complications. Here are some additional considerations:

- Never place yourself in a situation where a parent/guardian arrives for pickup, only to find their child is not at your program. Parents/guardians should always know the location of their child.
- Always have written permission to take enrolled children in your vehicle. Update those permissions as required. Parents/guardians should know and approve of your schedule.
- Always do repeated head counts and thoroughly double-check the vehicle when you leave it.
- Never leave children unattended.
- Carry emergency information and signed permissions for each child.
- Bring a cell phone and first aid kit including emergency medications.

- Make sure you understand what your insurance allows.
- BE SURE YOU UNDERSTAND ALL REGULATORY AND LEGAL REQUIREMENTS.

Do not overextend yourself. You may be complying with your quota, but taking children off the child care premises may require an additional set of hands and eyes. Don't overestimate what you are able to control.

PRODUCT SAFETY

Operating your program in a proactive manner takes on special importance when ensuring the safety of your early child care equipment and materials. Faulty equipment poses a very real threat in early child care facilities. Among children under four years of age, unintentional injuries such as drowning, suffocation, and choking remain leading causes of accidental deaths. Far too many of these deaths occur when children are placed in products intended to protect them from harm, such as cribs, carriages, or bath seats. Many deaths are the result of strangulation or suffocation caused by faulty equipment. Proving a serious injury or death is the result of faulty equipment, rather than possible provider negligence, can be an expensive and often uphill battle. Understanding product liability, protecting your business, and most importantly, ensuring the safety of children in your program must be a primary concern when obtaining materials and equipment.

Although the CPSC advocates for manufacturers to post all recall information on the manufacturer's website, currently many companies do not post updated or complete lists. In some instances, a product may have accumulated reported incidents, including deaths, without the product being placed on a recall list at the time you make an inquiry. If you have or are about to acquire a piece of equipment and would like to find out whether incidents have been reported, CPSC will send you detailed information. If you need information on more than one brand, submit a separate inquiry for each brand.

Protecting the children in your care is the best way to protect your business. Before purchasing any equipment for your child care facility, do your homework. For example, the state of California has a website that deals specifically with cancer-causing agents present in some equipment. The following websites are good places to search for reliable child safety information:

- American Academy of Pediatrics: www.aap.org
- California's Proposition 65 Warnings: www.p65warnings.ca.gov
- Consumer Product Safety Commission: www.cpsc.gov
- National Highway Traffic Safety Administration (for car seat recommendations and correct installation): www.nhtsa.gov

Manufacturers have a responsibility to notify consumers who have submitted registration cards if their product is recalled. If your equipment was not purchased new or you do not have a manufacturer's registration card, you can create one and mail it to the company. You can download the following Product Registration Card by scanning this QR code or visiting www.redleafpress.org/pyb/1-2.pdf.

PRODUCT REGISTRATION CARD

NAME: _____

TELEPHONE NUMBER: _____

EMAIL ADDRESS: _____

ADDRESS: _____

CITY: _____

STATE: _____ ZIP CODE: _____

PRODUCT BRAND MANUFACTURER: _____

PRODUCT MODEL NUMBER: _____

SIGNATURE: _____ DATE: _____

(Remember to photocopy this card and keep a copy for your file.)

STAFF

Do you have people working or volunteering in your program (including house-hold members and friends)? If so, please remember it's your business and "the buck stops with you." Innumerable cases exist in which a provider's license has been put in jeopardy because of an action taken by someone working or assist-ing in a program. Like all regulations, be sure you understand the require-ments in your state about your use of assistants/volunteers. You can't assume that someone else's actions or inactions will not affect your license.

If it's not already required by regulation, create an Approved Assistant Log that allows you to check off each requirement for individual employees.

- Employee/assistant/volunteer is current with all regulatory requirements:
  - Picture ID
  - All required background checks
  - Current license or certification (as applicable)
  - CPR and first aid certification/training (when required)
  - Proof of required training requirements
  - Current physical
  - Other
- Employee/Assistant/Volunteer Signature Sheet acknowledging their understanding of all regulations and policies, including but not limited to:
  - Appropriate supervision
  - Safe sleep guidelines and regulatory requirements
  - Ratio/quota requirements
  - Appropriate behavior management strategies
- Employee/assistant/volunteer can identify all attending children by their first and last names.
- Employee/assistant/volunteer knows the location of and can easily access all required information:
  - Individual child care records
  - Attendance logs for children and staff
  - Evacuation logs

- Approved exits
- Emergency contact information for all children and staff
- Identity of all individuals preapproved to pick up children
- The location of their own personnel file
- Your contact information when you are absent from the program

Additional tips:

- Anyone assisting or employed in your program should participate in at least one emergency evacuation practice every six months.
- Regardless of your state's regulations about picture IDs, it is strongly recommended that you require a picture ID for volunteers, assistants, and employees. It allows you to demonstrate, if questioned, that the individual working with you is the same individual whose name appears on any paperwork.
- As anyone who works in child care quickly realizes, temperament is important. An individual can have all the credentials in the world and still be uncomfortable with children. Finding qualified staff and assistants can sometimes be challenging. Keep in mind, however, that someone ill suited for child care can cause real damage to your reputation and your business. Consider probationary periods before you hire.
- If family members are assisting in your business, the temperament recommendation is the same. Having an assistant may allow you to increase your enrollment. Although there may be a lot of positives to having the extra help, if the individual you choose does not have the temperament or desire to work with children, your decision may result in a less than positive outcome.

"Regularly on the Premises"

Because of new background check requirements, make sure that anyone not residing in your home or no longer regularly on the premises is not using your address. If anyone using your address has a criminal issue, the burden may fall on you to prove they do not live at or regularly visit your home. In many states this includes hours even when your child care is not open. Proving someone using your address is not a household member or is not regularly on the premises can be difficult. Young adults away at college or in the military who continue to use your address as their mailing address need to be reminded that any criminal behavior can affect your business. Ask questions about how your state interprets "regularly on the premises." Remember to report to your licensor all changes in household composition as they occur.

Occasionally I have been consulted on cases where a provider feels they are being asked to choose between their business and their family. This is always difficult. However, every licensed provider needs to acknowledge that there are requirements they must adhere to in order to maintain a license. One of those requirements deals with required criminal background checks. I have seen providers surrender their license in order to provide shelter to a son, daughter, or partner who is experiencing challenges. This is obviously a difficult and personal decision. However, because you are operating a business in your home, the worst decision is to attempt to hide the fact that someone who is disqualified because of background information is living in your home or regularly visiting the premises. You open yourself up to potential liability. It has been my experience that this type of situation rarely ends well for the provider.

CUSTODY ISSUES

You may have enrolled children whose parents are divorced or currently separated. Parents, guardians, and providers need to understand that a provider cannot simply take the word of one parent over another, regardless of who is paying for the child care arrangement. In the case of children who are fostered, ensure that you have all the required documentation. If custody has been established by a court, make sure you have a copy of any legal documents that restrict or clarify access to the child during child care hours. If a restraining order is in place, for example, a copy of that order should be included in the child's file. In the majority of states, before a court has made a ruling, both parents have the right to access their child while in your care. Make sure everyone working in your program understands who has approved access and who does not. The following website provides some guidelines for releasing children in the event of potential custody issues. If you have additional questions or are concerned about potential liability, seek legal advice.

- Guidelines for Releasing Children and Potential Custody Issues: https://publiccounsel.org/wp-content/uploads/2021/12/Guidelines-for-Releasing-Children-Updated-May-2010.pdf

If you are currently involved in a divorce or separation or have filed for a restraining order, request language that prohibits your estranged spouse/partner from interfering with your ability to operate your business. That language should include prohibitions on making false accusations or filing unfounded complaints. Unfortunately, it is not uncommon for an estranged spouse to use your business as a way to retaliate or attempt to gain leverage in custody or financial disputes. As you move forward and consult with an attorney or a court representative, make sure you request specific wording that provides as much protection as possible for you and your business.

V. Professionalizing Your Program

Always remember that you are a professional, and conduct your business accordingly. Managing your program as a business, keeping good documentation and records, and advocating for yourself and the field can all contribute to your success.

DEVELOP YOUR BUSINESS SKILLS

To be successful, providers are responsible not only for the appropriate care of children but also for the appropriate management of their small businesses. The skill set necessary to be a good caregiver does not always include the same skills necessary to be a successful business owner. For example, because most states are now requiring online submission of information, computer literacy has become a necessary skill. Many providers find themselves depending on others, including household members, to assist them when they need to use their computers. This is not always a good business plan. Although computer literacy is not usually a requirement for a license, the more you know, the easier new expectations become.

In addition, operating a profitable business in a tightly regulated and competitive industry can be a real challenge. Access to reliable business management information has become increasingly important. Avoiding potential problems that can occur as a result of faulty record keeping as well as potential tax or liability issues is always in your best interest.

These examples represent two types of expertise (computer literacy and business management) that are frequently overlooked when providers are choosing workshops or degree programs. It's to your advantage to broaden your expertise. Do not neglect skill development that allows you to be a successful businessperson.

DOCUMENT EVERYTHING

You are busy. It's easy to understand why many providers are reluctant to take on another task. However, having well-organized and accurate documentation may save you a lot of money and headaches. Family child care providers frequently work alone. In many instances, your communication is one-on-one. Having a record you can refer to that reflects what was said as well as what actually occurred provides you with some protection.

If you ask questions and receive answers, make sure you maintain a record that accurately reflects what you were told. Keeping good documentation that allows you easy access to how you've been instructed to operate your business is a great example of how professionalizing your program can provide additional protection. Try to get your answers in writing. Request email or text confirmation when possible. Don't shortchange your program by avoiding interaction with your licensor.

It's important to take accurate notes that are both legible and understandable. Don't limit your note taking to licensing interactions; document any conversation that can affect your program, such as conversations with food program representatives, child care families, system monitors, and so on. Those of you who have challenged a citation or appealed an agency decision know the value of keeping accurate records. Your notes should not contain personal attacks or exaggerated embellishments but rather reveal an accurate representation of what occurred. Effective note taking requires some practice. Here are some things you can do to make this task easier:

- Always make sure you have something accessible to write on and with. For example, use your Monitoring Visit Log (see pp. 13–15).
- Set the pace of the conversation. Let the person you're speaking to know your intention to take notes. Don't be afraid to slow things down if you are unable to keep up.
- Don't feel like you need to write every word and every observation. For example, when speaking to a licensor, document any new information. You should also document anything that occurs that can affect your license or your reputation.
- Document anything you are instructed to do that is different or contradicts previous instruction you've been given.
- When given conflicting instructions, ask questions and document answers.
- Ask questions such as "Do I understand this is what you said?" to double-check the accuracy of your notes.
- Make sure you are able to read and understand your notes if using your own shorthand.
- Don't be afraid to ask questions. If, for example, you are cited because the licensor feels your food prep area is "cluttered," request the licensor describe specifically which items they consider "clutter" (this would have been helpful to Anne) and include their response in your notes. Having specific information about someone's interpretation of "clutter" is important if you decide to challenge the citation.
- Write down examples as needed. When I'm asked to present workshops to licensors, I remind them that it's necessary when making an assessment such as "unsanitary conditions" to include specific examples that support their assessment. The same rule holds true for providers. If you feel a citation is inaccurate or if you have reason to believe that you are being treated unfairly, you need specific examples to justify why you feel this way. It's not enough to say, "I am challenging this citation because I don't agree, and my licensor doesn't like me." You need, through the help of your documentation, to be able to support your conclusions with specific examples.

BE YOUR OWN BEST ADVOCATE

If you don't speak up for yourself, who will? The following are tips for getting involved in the field on a professional level and becoming your own best advocate:

- Be proactive. Most states, before new regulations are enacted, offer a period set aside for public feedback. Find out the schedule for public hearings and try to participate. If you can't attend, ask where and how to submit a comment.
- If you are not currently involved in a provider support group, consider joining one. If there are no support groups close to you, consider starting one. Child care can be isolating. Make opportunities to discuss common issues with other providers.
- Don't be shy. This is your business. You have the right to expect accountability from the agencies and individuals who oversee your program. Don't be hesitant to hold other professionals accountable in a respectful and productive way. For example, politely asking a licensor or home visitor to sign and date your documentation at the conclusion of a visit is not rude; it's good business.
- See if you can participate in state-organized committees. Many of these committees focus on new regulations; find out if you can sit on a committee. If that type of participation is not something you have the will or the time to do, identify which providers sit on those committees, and reach out to them with any concerns or comments you have.
- See if there is a union representing early child care providers in your state. If there is, ask what type of representation, as well as other benefits, union membership can provide. Are you affiliated with any national organizations that provide advocacy for family and group child care providers? Your voice is stronger when combined with others.
- Because you need to be able to read and understand regulations, if you require translated materials, it's important for you to have access to them. Reach out to your regulatory agency, union, other providers, support groups, child care systems, resource and referral agencies (R&Rs),

political representatives, and concerned families. Do whatever you can to ensure that appropriately translated licensing materials are available.

- Many states introduced "emergency requirements and guidelines" that clarified what was necessary to remain open during the COVID-19 pandemic. When temporary changes are introduced, it's always a good idea to get something in writing that you can share with your child care families. Don't leave yourself vulnerable to potential complaints or liability.

IMPLEMENT STRATEGIES THAT SUPPORT A PROACTIVE EARLY CHILD CARE PROGRAM

If nothing else, understand that on any given day your ability to provide child care could be jeopardized. That does not mean that you provide inferior care or even that you intentionally did anything wrong. It means that it's important to understand the vulnerabilities of your profession. You purchase insurance not because you believe your house will burn down but because you need to be prepared *if* your house is on fire. Developing a proactive business model allows you to stay prepared regardless of what occurs. Consider the following suggestions to ensure that you are building a proactive business model:

- Choose workshops that will help you protect your business. Many providers find themselves in trouble because of what they don't know. If your licensing agency provides training to clarify regulations or policies, try to take advantage of those opportunities. If your licensing authority does not make that type of training available, request it.
- Always remember that you are operating a business, regardless of its size. In many states, liability insurance is a requirement of licensure. In a majority of cases, your homeowner's or rental insurance will not cover issues that are related to your home-based business. Make sure you understand the legal and regulatory requirements in your state, and consider purchasing family child care liability insurance, whether or not it's a regulatory requirement. For example, some insurance coverage will provide you with an attorney if you find yourself in legal jeopardy

associated with your child care program. Some unions, family child care support groups, or private organizations provide access to reduced-cost insurance as a benefit of membership. Talk with other providers and collect information. Shop around to find the best arrangement for you.

- Don't wait to search for legal advice or advocacy when you need it. It's a much better idea to do your homework and have a plan in place. The time to locate an attorney or advocate is before you need one. You should investigate potential costs and identify attorneys and/or advocates with relevant experience. This is important because regulatory law is unique. Some providers do not see the need for this type of planning because they are certain they will never need an attorney or advocate. Unfortunately, you could easily be left without appropriate representation when and if you need it.

- Proactively create a rainy-day fund. Saving a little each week or month is usually much easier than attempting to cover the cost of an attorney on short notice. I have spoken to many providers who were able to put away a sufficient sum to offset the cost of any mandated closures.

- Survey families quarterly to collect references and positive feedback, rather than waiting until after a complaint has been filed. Not only does this allow you to receive and maintain family feedback, but it also provides readily available written testimony you can share with investigators whenever necessary. It is also helpful because it gives families a professional option to share any issues or concerns. This approach lets you address potential problems before they escalate. You can download the following Sample Family Survey by scanning this QR code or visiting www.redleafpress.org/pyb/1-3.pdf.

SAMPLE FAMILY SURVEY

Parent/Guardian Name: _____ Date: _____

What parts of our daily routine do you and your child most enjoy? _____

_____

_____

Do you and/or your child have issues or concerns about any aspect of the

child care program? _____

_____

Do you feel there are sufficient opportunities for communication? _____

_____

_____

Do you have suggestions about how we can adjust or improve our child care

service to better meet the needs of you and your children? _____

_____

_____

_____

- Periodically check required records. Make sure your training hours, CPR and first aid certification, background checks, and required physical are all current. If you employ assistants, double-check to ensure that their paperwork is complete. Review your child care records carefully. Don't enroll children before receiving the required paperwork. Review your attendance records for accuracy on a daily basis.

- Periodically check to make sure there haven't been changes to your state's regulations and policies. States often take the position that because it's your business, it's your responsibility to identify rule changes. Do yourself a favor and find out where and how to obtain information about regulatory and requirement changes. It's much better to be safe than sorry. Remember, saying you didn't know rarely excuses you from getting a citation or something worse.

- Try to see unannounced licensing visits as an opportunity to ask questions, get clarification, and use your Monitoring Visit Log. So often providers tell me it's almost impossible to hear anything a licensor is saying during a monitoring visit because it's at that moment children in the program inevitably begin to act up. If you are nervous about the visit, it's only natural that children pick up on how you're feeling. Every state has a regulatory requirement to practice emergency evacuation monthly. I recommend that you also regularly practice what to do when an adult visits your program during child care hours. It's helpful to have a "quiet box" where children can find "special" materials to use for these occasions. You still have an obligation to supervise during the visit, and this strategy may not always offer you a great deal of time, depending on the ages of the children, but it does work. I have seen providers use this technique successfully, and it's amazing to see little children so prepared when an adult visits their child care!

VI. Questions from the Field

During the many years I've worked as a consultant, I've talked with thousands of providers throughout the United States. The following information is a compilation of common questions I've heard.

My licensor hates me. What can I do?

Unfortunately, this is no joke. Former providers have told me that this is part of the reason they left the profession. Ask yourself why you feel your licensor "hates" you. When you have a moment, sit down and make a list. If your list contains a majority of items that deal primarily with personality, for example, "She doesn't smile enough" or "She never has anything positive to say," it might help to talk with your licensor about how you feel. In an effort to maintain their professionalism, some licensors are unaware of how they may come across. Many licensors use templates/checklists during a monitoring visit, and those lists often do not mention positive feedback. As a result, licensors are sometimes inclined to believe that as long as you don't have any violations, you should be satisfied that the visit went well. Using your own Monitoring Visit Log may help. If by the end of a licensing visit your licensor has not given you any positive feedback, don't be afraid to ask. It's perfectly appropriate for you to ask your licensor to share any positive observations made during the visit. In some instances, licensors may respond by saying that they are unable to provide positive feedback because of their agency's policies. At least you will know it's not about you. However, you should document their response. In other instances, a licensor may respond with positive feedback. Make sure you include those comments in your log and request the licensor's signature at the conclusion of the visit.

Occasions may arise when the items on your list have nothing to do with personality differences. You may feel your licensor demonstrates bias, or you feel you are consistently harassed. You may feel the licensor visiting your program often exhibits incompetence or behaves in an unprofessional manner. The following list contains steps you can take to help alleviate some of those issues:

- Document, document, document! It is not enough for you to simply make allegations against a licensor. You need to be able to support your allegations. Make it a habit to document the dates and specifics of any licensing interactions, especially those interactions you feel were inappropriate. For example, if you feel you are being harassed, having documentation that demonstrates the number of unannounced visits and the duration of each visit is an effective way to support your position.

- Talk with other providers in your community. Are they having the same problems with the same licensor? If they are, you may want to submit information to your regulatory agency as a group. If you are a union member or a member of a provider support group, reach out for any information or support they can provide. If other providers tell you they do not have the same issues, that's also important information. It allows you to present a comparison. For example, if other providers receive an unannounced visit once a year and you are receiving unannounced visits quarterly, you certainly have the right to find out why this is occurring.

- If you feel your licensor does not have a good grasp of your state's regulations and the citations you receive are questionable, in your opinion, don't be afraid to seek a second opinion. As stated, citations should only be issued based on regulatory noncompliance, not on a licensor's personal opinion. Make sure you are able to demonstrate through your regulations, policy, or previous instruction why you believe a citation is inaccurate.

- Be proactive in operating your program by maintaining current contact information if you need to submit material to a supervisor or regional director for a second opinion. Obtain accurate contact information and agency procedures for challenging citations before you need to use it.

- Do not be fearful of retaliation. Licensors and state regulatory agencies have an obligation to act responsibly and can and should be held accountable when appropriate. If you are confident you have collected sufficient evidence to support your position, do not hesitate to bring your information to individuals at the administrative level of your licensing agency for a second review. In too many instances, providers feel vulnerable and disempow- ered. You are a provider who owns a business that is subject to licensure. Being licensed does not mean that you lose the right to defend yourself and your business—just do it professionally. This is especially important if you believe any allegations made against you are false.

> I believe strongly that young children learn through play. My daily routine is designed to allow participating children as much free time as possible. I have a new licensor who appears appalled at my approach to early child care. She has suggested that my daily routine is not purposeful and that what I describe as an effective strategy for early learning is actually an excuse for not providing adequate curriculum. She has told me that if I do not make altera- tions, I will be subject to formal licensing intervention. What can I do?

First of all, your knowledge regarding what is contained in your regu- lations is important. What do your regulations say about curriculum? Is there a corresponding policy about how you structure your daily routine? It is sometimes surprising to providers and to licensors how specific requirements regarding the inclusion of curriculum are not always available in family child care regulations. For example, your regulations may contain generic language that requires a variety of potential learning opportunities and various learning environments within your program. Often regulations do not offer much specific- ity regarding curriculum. Make sure you understand what your state

actually requires. Take a close look at your program so, when necessary, you can easily demonstrate how your daily routines meet those
requirements.

Many states have additional expectations above what's required
by regulation. If you provide care to children whose tuition is subsidized by your state, you may be subject to additional requirements,
often determined by independent or state-affiliated programs. In a
tiered reimbursement program, each tier level is attached to a corresponding amount of tuition reimbursement. Usually reimbursement increases as you advance in the system. To advance, a provider
often needs to meet benchmarks that include educational or training requirements or certification expectations. There can also be
expectations regarding the inclusion of specific curriculum and daily
routines. If your state has initiated this type of process, get information about how it affects you.

If you are using a "learn through play" framework, collect credible resources that support your perspective. Also, if you are asked
to demonstrate how your daily routines are purposeful, sharing your
objectives for each child and demonstrating how those objectives are
achieved through your curriculum will go a long way in making your
case.

If you are cited, make sure you are given the specific regulation
or policy that is used to justify the citation. Read it carefully, and if
you do not agree with your licensor's interpretation, challenge the
citation.

A child in my program was enrolled by her mother. The mother
signed the contract with me, filled out and signed the enrollment
packet, and reimburses me every week. She is the only contact
person listed. Recently I learned this child's parents are divorced.
The father, whom I had not met and who does not appear as a
contact, arrived unannounced at my program demanding to see his

child. He expressed his disapproval of my family child care program. I feel he may file a complaint against me just to make things
increasingly difficult for the mother. What can I do?

Speak with the child's mother. Make sure you have copies of all legal
paperwork that describes the custody arrangement. You should keep
a copy of that paperwork (schedules, restraining orders, any restrictions) in the child's file.

Contact your licensor to alert them to the situation; inquire about
the regulations regarding parental rights; and never assume that
because one parent is paying for child care, the other parent does
not have rights. For example, if this is a joint custody arrangement,
does the father need to sign all your permission forms along with the
mother? Parents may have differing opinions regarding your ability
to photograph the child, for example. Make sure you understand the
regulations and laws in your state regarding parental access. While
you may empathize with the situation, do not jeopardize your program by assuming legal authority that does not exist. Ensure that
anyone working in your program is aware of who has legal access to
any participating child.

I own and operate a group family child care home. I really love
what I do, and I have earned a good income from my business.
My problem is my own children. I have an older daughter in college and three children at home, two in middle school and one in
high school. My kids always enjoyed my child care before, but now
everything has changed. I was recently able to add an addition to
my home for my primary child care space. My kids seem to feel that
the additional space should be theirs so they can entertain their
friends. I've been accused of caring more about my business than I
care about my children. I am confused and hurt, and I really don't
know what I should do.

As someone who has lived with teenagers, I can sympathize. It's difficult even if you aren't operating a business in your home. However, everyone needs to be on the same page when your business and your family share the same environment.

Sometimes it's easy to assume that everyone living in your household should and will appreciate the benefits your business has provided. Unfortunately, that assumption is not always accurate. This may be a good time to have a family chat. Let your children know that you want their feedback, and that you really are interested in what they have to say. Try scheduling a family meeting when it is convenient for everyone, not just you, to attend. Encourage them to explain their issues to you, and be prepared to listen. Dealing with adolescent family members can often require more negotiation skills than working at the United Nations.

Before sitting down, think about ways that you may be able to compromise or accommodate their needs. You may also want to consider your bottom line and be prepared to explain why there are some circumstances that you are unable to adjust or compromise because of financial considerations, regulations, or the nature of your business.

Family meetings can often become heated. Keep a calm demeanor. Avoid drama whenever possible. Be willing to show that you want to work things out in a way that is satisfactory for everyone. Acknowledge that, in the end, everyone may not be happy, including you, but that it's an ongoing process and you want to keep the lines of communication open. Good luck!

HELP! I'M IN TROUBLE!

I HAVE CONSULTED WITH HUNDREDS OF PROVIDERS. I have participated as a provider advocate in licensing meetings and disciplinary hearings, negotiated agreements, and represented providers at appeal hearings. What is most distressing to me is the number of cases that could have been avoided.

As I present workshops, I always encounter at least one provider who tells me that proactive strategies are unnecessary in their program because they know the secret to managing their licensor. I have heard providers share their belief that their licensor wouldn't dare create problems. There are some providers who consistently believe that a good defense is a strong offense. On those occasions I try to respectfully remind the provider that there is a difference between assertiveness (which is a good thing) and aggressive behavior (which is not a good thing). Many providers inadvertently place a bull's-eye on their own backs by behaving in an overly aggressive and intimidating manner.

There is such an implied imbalance of power in the interactions between licensors and providers that it's easy to understand why so many providers feel defensive. Feeling defensive in your own home and business is never comfortable. It is certainly difficult to create a sense of collaboration when providers often feel their licensor is not there to help them but rather to catch them doing something wrong. Often when this type of tension builds over an extended period of time, if and when something does occur the issue can become a much bigger problem than it should.

You cannot control what your licensor thinks. Most licensors will do their job the way they believe it should be done. This means that sometimes their perspective may be in direct contradiction to yours. You only have control over your part of the interaction between you and your licensor. If an unintended issue does occur in your program, you will need all the support you can gather. You may have a bumpy history with your licensor. Your licensing history will play a role in any subsequent investigation. It's not necessary for you and your licensor to "like" each other, but it is helpful when you are able to respect each other. Perpetuating a divisive relationship does not usually work to your advantage, especially if there is an unintended incident that may require licensing intervention.

Section 1 covered the advantages of operating a proactive program. Section 2 focuses on what occurs if and when you do find yourself in trouble. Unfortunately, the providers who have experienced the most difficulties during this period are often the same providers who believed their programs were impervious to allegations or licensing intervention. This section is for every provider who owns and operates an early child care program, because any provider, at any time, can be the subject of licensing intervention.

I. Case Study Two

Sarah has been providing family child care for twenty-two years. Sarah began when her own children were small. She quickly discovered her small bedroom community was an excellent place to open a home-based child care business. In the twenty-two years she's been open, Sarah has always had full enrollment and has consistently been able to operate a profitable business. Sarah has stayed current with her regulations, and she maintains an appropriately professional relationship with her licensor. Until lately, she fortunately had never experienced any real problems and was happy with her career choice.

Recently, Sarah's husband, Tim, was offered early retirement. Tim was a great help in Sarah's child care. He enjoyed children, was great with their grandchildren, and was well liked by all of Sarah's child care clients. So when this opportunity arose, it seemed a natural choice to have Tim assist Sarah in her child care program on a full-time basis. Tim submitted all the required paperwork and was approved to assist Sarah with no difficulty.

They had been working together for a while, and it was better than Sarah expected. Having an extra set of eyes and hands had proven to be a real plus, and they had discussed applying to increase their quota. But everything abruptly changed the morning Sarah received a call from her licensor. She was told a complaint had been filed against her program on behalf of a child for physical abuse. Sarah was horrified. How could anyone think that she could or would hurt a child? As it turned out, the complaint concerning abuse was not against Sarah but against Tim. It was alleged that Tim "roughly grabbed a child by the thigh, leaving a significant bruise."

The licensor went on to state that an investigation would be conducted by a representative from the licensing agency, as well as an investigator representing the social service agency, the Department of Social Services (DSS). The DSS had oversight when there was an allegation of abuse and neglect. The licensor further stated that the allegation had been forwarded by DSS to the district attorney's office for further review. As a result of that referral, Sarah was informed there might also be a police presence as part of the investigation. In addition, the licensor said that if the investigation determined Tim was responsible for the child's injury, then Sarah would most probably be determined negligent. If that occurred, both Sarah and Tim would automatically be disqualified from providing child care.

If all of that were not bad enough, Sarah was informed that she needed to cease providing child care immediately until the investigation was completed and there was a final determination. Sarah was told to call each of her child care clients to pick up their children immediately and to let them know her program would be closed until further notice.

When the call ended, Sarah could not move. She couldn't get her mind around what had just occurred. Although Sarah believed she had stayed current with her regulations, she found herself totally unaware of the legal power of her licensing agency. Could they really close her just like that? Sarah had always done what she was instructed to do regarding her license. In addition, she had a good working relationship with her child care families, and she had a very good licensing history. How was it possible she could be closed during a five-minute telephone conversation?

Then Sarah thought about the calls she needed to make to her child care families requesting they immediately pick up their children. What should she tell them? Should she share everything that she had just been told by her licensor, or should she tell them she and Tim had a family emergency and leave it at that? At this point, Sarah didn't know how long she would need to stay closed. How was she supposed to explain an undetermined closure to families who depended on her and would certainly ask questions?

Sarah talked with Tim, and they decided they would not share specific information with their child care families until they fully understood what had just happened. The child pickups were not pleasant. Sarah and Tim contracted with working families who depended on them to be reliable caregivers. It was extremely difficult to come up with an explanation for why they were closing so suddenly and why they were unable to tell families how long they would be closed. Families were not happy, children were not happy, and neither were Sarah and Tim.

Later that afternoon and well into the night, Sarah and Tim kept going over what happened. Tim was adamant that he had never knowingly injured a child. Nor did he believe that he had ever handled or "roughly" touched anyone. Sarah believed him. They spent many hours trying to determine who might have filed this complaint. They finally decided it must have been the parent of their most recent enrollee. The child was an active two-year-old, and it was apparent that the mother had little control over his behavior at drop-off or pickup time. This was a child Tim spent a lot of time with during the day. Tim frequently engaged with three toddlers during child care hours. This gave Sarah an opportunity to introduce more structured activities with the older children without unnecessary distractions. Tim was very fond of this particular child, and it really hurt him to think that anyone would believe he could injure this little boy.

As the seriousness of all of this began to sink in, it was hard not to panic. Sarah and Tim had lived in their small community for a long time. This was not only scary but incredibly embarrassing. What would happen to their reputation? What would their friends, their neighbors, and their family think?

Could this turn into a criminal situation? Because they felt they knew who filed the complaint, should they try to contact the mother and demand to know why she did this? (Reminder: It is never a good idea to assume who filed a complaint. You may be incorrect in your assumption, and accusing someone without evidence could create a worse situation.) Sarah and Tim had an attorney they used for estate planning. Should they try to contact him in the morning? How long would this whole thing take? Who would have access to this allegation? What could be the long-term consequences if the investigation did not vindicate them? They had so many questions and no easy answers. What should they do?

DISCUSSION

As in Case Study One, the information contained in this case study is based on actual events. Every day, licensed providers all over the United States are exposed to situations like this one. While it's true that individual states have their own unique protocol, the events in this example accurately reflect what can and does occur in most states when this type of allegation is made against a family child care program.

In section 1, we discussed the advantages of operating your program proactively to avoid potential licensing intervention. In section 2, we will focus on what happens when you find yourself in trouble. The questions asked by Sarah and Tim are good ones. Do you know the answers?

Let's examine some of the issues that may arise during the operation of your program.

II. Citations

A *citation* is formal notification of a regulatory violation. For example, if a licensor visits your program and finds that a required gate is not in place, you may be cited for violating the regulation that requires appropriate barriers. Citations can also be called *violations* or *noncompliances*. It can help to know the answers to the following questions about citations if your program receives one.

What if you make the correction to a noncompliance while the licensor is still in your program?

A lot depends on the licensing procedures in your state. If the non-compliance does not pose an immediate or serious threat to the safety of children, a licensor may have the discretion to allow you to immediately make the correction without citing you.

In many states, however, licensors are required to write the citation, regardless of whether you're able to make the correction during the visit. Ask what the policy is in your state. Knowing whether a written citation is discretionary may prove important to your licensing profile in the future.

If you are cited despite making the correction, make sure the correction is reflected on the licensor's visit report, as well as the time and date the correction was made. Document your correction on your Monitoring Visit Log and ask your licensor to sign and date your documentation before they leave your program—but remember that you cannot force someone to sign. Act professionally. If a licensor refuses to sign, politely inform the licensor that you will be documenting their refusal.

Once corrected, do citations go away?

In most states, your citation history is usually accessible for as long as you retain your license. The fact that a citation no longer appears on a website does not mean the citation has been removed from your licensing history. The National Association of Regulatory Agencies recently sponsored a workshop discussing the possibility of reviewing noncompliance data to determine future licensing initiatives. Find out what the practice is in your state for redacting information from your licensing profile. Many states post providers' licensing profiles (including citations and any licensing restrictions) on their websites.

At the very least, every licensed provider should check their state's official website at least once a year. Just like checking your credit report, you can only correct misinformation if you know it's there. Ask about the type of information your licensing authority needs to make corrections to your licensing profile. You should also ask about the expected time frame to get information corrected. Don't neglect to follow up.

What's the big deal? Everyone gets citations.

While it's true that most early child care professionals receive a citation every now and then, the frequency, volume, and severity of citations can affect your business. You may have a reasonable explanation for every citation, but someone reading your licensing history may not see or hear your explanation. Because a prospective client visiting your state's website may have access to your citations without context, they may come away with a negative impression. Often when I advocate for providers at licensing meetings or appeal hearings, providers are surprised to find individuals on the opposite side of the table with pages of information. Many providers incorrectly assume that once a citation is corrected, everything is forgiven and forgotten. It has been my experience that nothing in your licensing history is forgotten, especially when something occurs in your program that requires licensing intervention. Your citation history has relevance in ways you may not expect. As Anne from section 1 moves forward and she is visited again, all the information collected during that infamous visit will be available to any subsequent licensing representative. Organizing and operating your business in a way that helps you avoid citations is always to your advantage. This is especially true in our current environment where information is easily collected and stored.

What should you do if you disagree with a citation?

A citation should never be issued because of a licensor's personal opinion. A citation should only be issued in response to a regulatory violation. When you disagree with a citation, your knowledge of the regulations should work to your advantage. Always have a copy of your regulations readily available when you're caring for children. During a visit, a licensor needs to be able to show you the regulation or policy referred to in the citation. If after reading the regulation or policy you believe your licensor's interpretation is incorrect, respectfully tell them why you disagree. Any documentation you have (previous visit reports, Monitoring Visit Logs or relevant policy, resource, or technical assistance material) are all good ways to underscore your position. If your licensor is adamant about their interpretation, you need to respectfully request the name and contact information of their supervisor. Let the licensor know your intention to submit information for review and a second opinion. You have the right to protect your business. You have a right to challenge citations. But you must do it professionally!

III. Complaints and Investigations

There is nothing more nerve-racking than hearing that you or someone involved with your program is on the receiving end of a complaint. This is especially true for providers who have convinced themselves that this can happen only to someone else. Understand that regardless of how long you've been licensed and no matter the nature of your relationship with your licensor, you can never assume that simply because you deny any wrongdoing you will automatically be given the benefit of the doubt. I have met many providers who feel disillusioned and personally betrayed during investigations. Don't allow that to happen to you. It's a distraction at a time when you need to stay focused.

There is not a lot a provider can do to prevent someone who wants to from making allegations. However, you can do things that can help you protect your business if false or misleading allegations are made. If a complaint has been filed against your program, it's not too late to help yourself. Consider the following strategies if you find yourself in this situation:

- First, don't panic—get motivated. Unfortunately, embarrassment, disbelief, and fear are some reasons many providers find themselves unprepared when a complaint investigation occurs. If you are currently in that situation, please remember that any provider, at any time, can become the subject of an investigation. Having a complaint filed against your program that results in an investigation does not automatically mean you did something wrong.

- Follow the same tips for avoiding citations as they are also relevant when avoiding complaints. One of the most effective ways to avoid negative consequences is to demonstrate that you consistently operate your program in compliance with your state's regulations. Accidents happen—however, if you are operating an early child care program, a determination of fault will usually be decided on whether you were following your regulations when the incident occurred. The challenge for you will be to demonstrate how a child was injured despite your compliance with your regulations.

- Keep past Monitoring Visit Logs and other notes organized and accessible. Maintain any training or professional development credentials, Family Surveys, and references in an organized manner. This will allow you to easily share relevant information as quickly and professionally as possible.

- Do not leave yourself vulnerable by neglecting to document incidents that happen during the operation of your program. Many complaints come down to the credibility of the complainant against the credibility of the provider. Your thorough documentation of any incident can go a long way in substantiating your version of what actually occurred. Don't place yourself in a situation that gives a client reason not to trust you. Clients who lose trust are more likely to file complaints. Disclose any incidents as quickly and professionally as possible, and document everything.

- Don't limit documentation to incidents that occur with enrolled children. If you have a difference of opinion with a child care client, a family member, an ex, an employee, or a neighbor regarding the operation of your child care business, document, document, document!
- Take complaints seriously. A complaint investigation is not the end of the world, and it certainly does not guarantee an end to your business; however, it's something you should not ignore. Searching for reliable information about how investigations are conducted in your state before you are the subject of an investigation allows you to stay prepared. Collecting relevant information can also help to mitigate the damage that may result from a complaint investigation. Your preparation should include obtaining information about advocacy or union or legal representation that can help you sustain your business during and after your investigation. Having informed representation can assist with any subsequent legal action that may occur. It's helpful to keep in mind that many providers find themselves with a stronger business as a result of their experience.

HOUSEHOLD INVOLVEMENT

No one can sabotage your program as quickly or effectively as a household member. Allegations made by individuals who presumably have firsthand knowledge about you and the day-to-day operation of your program are usually taken very seriously. This also applies when household members are asked to share information during an investigation. Family members may not have been the ones to make allegations, but they can certainly bury you with their testimony. I have witnessed providers caught totally off guard when a household member or employee shared information that was damaging to the program and to the provider. No one wants to be taken for granted, and your household members are usually no exception.

Living in the same space where you operate your business poses a variety of challenges. For example, everyone needs to pitch in and clean up after themselves, as even small mistakes like curling irons or nail polish remover unintentionally left accessible on a bathroom counter can result in citations, or perhaps something worse if a child is injured. Everyone in your household must understand their role in the success of your business.

I once acted as an advocate for a provider during a complaint investigation. The allegation was that the provider's eleven-year-old son bullied the children in the program. The provider was adamant that her son never bullied any child in her care. I sat in on the questioning of the provider and her son. When questioned about bullying, the eleven-year-old immediately responded that "he had never bullied anyone." He was a cute kid, and his response was sincere. The investigator was experienced, so she changed her questioning from general behavior to specific incidents. She asked him if he had ever hit a child who participated in his mother's child care. She followed up her question by reminding him that it was important to tell the truth. He hesitated for a moment and then looked up and smiled and said, "Only in self-defense." When questioned about where the provider was when this occurred, he responded that "she wasn't around." Needless to say, the provider was horrified and things went downhill from that point.

When providers attend communication workshops, the focus is often limited to professional interactions, such as with potential child care clients or other professionals in the field. Those interactions are important—but so is your ability to communicate with your own family, especially when you operate a family child care business. An important goal is to make sure everyone is on the same page, which includes spouses, partners, young children, adolescents, and extended family. Also included are individuals who may no longer reside at your home but are still using your address for mail and/or identification. Providers can't assume that because they see and understand the value of their home-based business, everyone in their household shares the same perspective. Section 3 includes a detailed discussion about the value of interactive communication. In your attempt to create a proactive program, it's impossible to ignore what occurs in your own household. It does not mean your household members are required to lie on your behalf, but it does mean there should be a common understanding of what is required for you to operate a successful business. This understanding should include your responsibilities as well as theirs.

Be aware that individuals "regularly on the premises" may be subject to background checks and can affect your ability to maintain your license. Make sure you understand how "regularly on the premises" is defined in your state. Are days when you are not operating your program or areas of your home that are not part of your child care environment exempt from consideration when determining "regularly on the premises"? In many states they are not. Find out exactly what the rules are in your state. Don't guess or make false assumptions! Although it's your home, you are subject to regulations. If you do find yourself in a situation where, because of the criminal background information of someone who lives in your household or is regularly on the premises, your licensing agency has an issue, it's unwise to try to hide or distort the truth. The situation will only get worse. You may be asked to make difficult choices. If you do agree to disallow that individual from the premises, understand that if you compromise that agreement, in most instances you will jeopardize your ability to maintain your license. I strongly recommend that you get reliable advice before you sign any agreement that can affect your ability to continue to provide child care.

How you structure your program and how you decide to integrate your family and your business is your decision. However, to protect and professionalize your business, you need to consistently reinforce your expectations. Please keep in mind that your five-year-old who loved the fact that you were providing child care may have a very different opinion when he or she becomes twelve or thirteen. Make sure you are listening as well as communicating your expectations.

TYPES OF INVESTIGATIONS

The following is information related to specific types of investigations, including criminal investigations, social service investigations, food program investigations, and licensing investigations.

Criminal Investigations

If you have faced or are facing an issue that includes criminal allegations, you may already be aware that your criminal investigation usually includes notification to your licensing authority. If you become aware of any pending criminal or legal action against you, a household member, or an employee, notify your licensor. In most states, self-reporting is a regulatory requirement. It's always to your benefit to be on record as having self-reported any investigation that could affect your child care license. Because you and all those living in your household are subject to background checks, be sure you understand how allegations or convictions unrelated to child care can negatively affect you and your business. You should also be aware that juvenile records that are traditionally sealed may be available to agencies conducting background checks on providers and household members. If you are made aware that there are issues resulting from a background check, a criminal indictment, or an arrest, consider consulting an attorney. Make sure that you understand your legal rights and all of your options before making any major decisions, such as surrendering your license. Due to fear and potential embarrassment, many providers make impulsive decisions. It was wise for Sarah and Tim to consult with an attorney before their investigation was underway. Their estate attorney referred them to another attorney who specialized in their type of case.

Social Service Investigations

In most situations, in a majority of states any allegation that includes the non-accidental abuse and neglect of children is handled by your state's social service agency (Department of Children and Families, Child Protective Services, or Department of Social Services). In some states, the responsible agency may be the same agency that oversees your license. You need to understand which agency is responsible because, in most states, early child care providers are mandated reporters. This means that if you have concerns regarding a child who may have been abused or neglected, you have a legal responsibility to notify the responsible agency. As in criminal investigations, it is advisable to self-report to your licensing authority if you or someone in your program or household is alleged to have abused or neglected a child (including your own child). In most states, self-reporting allegations of abuse and neglect is also a regulatory requirement. Occasions may arise, based on the allegation, when subsequent investigation will include law enforcement, social service representatives, and representatives from your licensing authority. In instances when a referral has been made to a district attorney, it is advisable to obtain legal advice as soon as possible. If it's determined that you were responsible for the abuse and/or neglect, you will be given information about how to file an appeal. If you lose your appeal, you may be able to appeal that administrative decision in Superior Court in some states. Make sure you understand all of your options before making any decision that will affect your long-term ability to provide child care.

Food Program Investigations

Generally food program investigations are conducted when there are suspicions or allegations of fraud. You need to carefully read any contract with your food program before you sign it, and you should know how a negative food program decision might affect your license. Make it a practice to ask questions. In most states, food programs share information with licensing agencies. If the allegations against you are based on inaccurate enrollment or billing numbers, frequently a provider can expect agencies to cross-reference data. Keep all your records organized and available so that you can demonstrate that your attendance and billing numbers are accurate.

Licensing Investigations

Licensing investigations can occur after information is obtained from another state, federal, or private agency. They can also occur after an incident or when a serious issue is raised during a licensing visit. Most commonly, however, licensing investigations occur following allegations made against a provider or a program. In some instances, because of the specifics of an allegation, there may be joint investigations (representatives from more than one agency sharing information and resources). Keep in mind that a licensing investigation provides you with an opportunity to tell your side of the story. Remember that allegations are unsubstantiated accusations. If you are a union member, contact your union representative immediately. Again, do not make any major decisions until you fully understand all your options. Don't allow yourself to feel pressured into making decisions that may not be in your best interest. Get reliable advice!

DURING A COMPLAINT INVESTIGATION

Once a complaint investigation is underway, you can take several steps to help improve your outcomes.

Gather Positive References

In cases for which investigations are scheduled in advance, use time before the visit to request references from people who know you and have experience with your program. If you are already using a Family Survey, you should have positive references readily available. If not, quickly obtain as many positive references as you can. In Case Study Two, Sarah and Tim decided not to inform their child care clients that a complaint had been filed. They did this because they were unaware that all families of enrolled children are usually interviewed as part of an ongoing investigation. Unfortunately, rather than being informed by Sarah and Tim, families were informed by a stranger about the real reason their child care had to close. Parents/guardians who trusted their providers were confused at hearing they had not been told the truth. (Reminder: Don't underestimate the broad reach of an abuse investigation, and don't underestimate the support your child care families may provide when told the truth about an investigation.) It's always to your advantage, if you believe you have not done anything wrong, to simply tell the truth.

Get Organized

Gather copies of previous licensor visit logs, your Monitoring Visit Logs, and any monitoring reports created by other professionals who monitor your program. Organize information that helps demonstrate the appropriate way you operate your program. For example, if you have developed internal policies describing how you supervise or what your behavior management procedures are, you can share that information with the investigator. Carefully check your child care environment to ensure compliance with regulations. Don't assume investigators will focus only on the allegations in the complaint. Usually individuals investigating a program look at everything. Don't allow additional unrelated issues to be included in your complaint investigation.

Breathe

Being involved in an investigation can be extremely stressful. It's natural to feel nervous and defensive. Unfortunately, those feelings can lead to statements that are not in your best interest. Try very hard not to panic. Always think before you speak. Try not to ramble because you're nervous. Always answer questions truthfully and simply. Don't allow yourself to feel pressured. You are entitled to sufficient time to think before you respond. You are also entitled to sufficient time to take notes. Make sure you collect as much information as possible about the allegations made against your program. Sometimes investigators are reluctant to share too much information because they believe providers will contact potential witnesses and affect the outcome of their testimony. Don't get discouraged. If you make inquiries about the specifics of allegations and the investigator refuses to share that information, carefully document your question and the investigator's refusal. All aspects of an investigation may be relevant if you have to appeal the final determination. Try to stay calm and focus on taking accurate notes. If children are present during the investigation, make sure you are given adequate time to address the needs of each child.

Because Sarah and Tim worked together, Sarah was able to document what occurred during the investigation, leaving Tim the opportunity to respond to questions. It may be helpful for you to consider having someone else present during an investigation to provide support. If you have consulted with your union representative, an advocate, or an attorney, they will advise you regarding your options.

Listen Carefully

Frequently when people are nervous, they talk a lot and don't listen enough. Understand exactly what you've been accused of. You need to listen carefully so that when you do respond to a question, you have a clear understanding of what has been asked. If you do not understand a question, say so. Don't guess; ask for clarification. On those occasions when you don't have an answer, simply say you don't know. Always tell the truth. Do not attempt to create a response based solely on what you think the investigator wants to hear.

Document Everything

You will notice that this is a common theme throughout this guide. There's a reason for that. Your documentation can become a useful tool if you find it necessary to appeal a negative decision. You shouldn't place yourself in a situation where the only documentation available at the hearing is theirs and not yours. If you keep a Monitoring Visit Log, you can use it during an investigation. Document the date and time of arrival and the time of departure of investigators visiting your program. Record the names and contact information of everyone present. If the investigation visit is unannounced, make sure you understand the purpose of the visit at the time of entry. As in all professional visits, respectfully request that visitors sign your documentation before leaving the premises. If they refuse, document their refusal, and be sure that you understand all the allegations. If you are confused about what you actually have been accused of, ask questions until you understand the answers.

Do Not Obsess about Who May Have Filed a Complaint

In most states, a complainant's identity is protected. You are wasting time if all your energy is spent attempting to discover who complained. In Sarah and Tim's case, for example, the parent they assumed had filed the complaint was not actually the parent who made the allegation. If your goal in discovering the identity of the complainant is to discredit that person and redirect the focus of the investigation, be careful about how you proceed. Like Sarah and Tim, you may be wrong about the source of the complaint. Also, if you attempt to discredit a parent, for example, by sharing information you feel is damaging to their credibility, be prepared for backlash. Inevitably the first question will be, if you had prior knowledge regarding a parent's inappropriate behavior, why didn't you file a report? You can share relevant observations or information that, in your opinion, may help explain why a complaint may have been filed, but never attempt to denigrate a child or a parent/guardian during an investigation. It just reflects poorly on you.

Know That Information Is Power

Understanding your rights (what they actually are, not what you assume they should be) offers you some leverage. It allows you to develop a realistic plan if an investigation should occur. One of the first steps you can take is to learn about the complaint procedures in your state. For example, in the case of a multiagency investigation, can you request separate meetings? This would have been very helpful information for Sarah and Tim. Although providers are often strongly tempted to get it all over with at once, that may not always be the wisest choice. Get good advice. For some providers, having two or three investigators in their program simultaneously can be overwhelming. If necessary, what about language interpretation? Is the responsible agency required to provide interpretation? Are you able to request that another person be present for support and advocacy during your investigation? Are you able to continue to provide child care during an open investigation? Can you negotiate the scheduling of an investigation? Collecting this type of information before you need it can help you stay prepared. If you are prepared, you place yourself in a much better position.

Ask Questions before Surrendering Your License

Depending on the allegations, agency representatives might encourage you to surrender your license. Try not to make such an important decision when you are in the midst of an investigation. Depending on your state's policies and the specifics of the complaint, surrendering your license may not make everything go away. For example, can the surrender of your license be equated to an admission of guilt? If so, how does that affect your liability? This is especially relevant in cases where a child has been unintentionally injured. You need to know what information will appear in your licensing record if you simply surrender your license. If you decide to apply for a new job, what type of information will be available to future employers? In some states you may be requested to formally "voluntarily" inactivate your license during an investigation. This usually involves signing an agreement that states you will be unable to operate your program while an investigation is ongoing. Ask questions regarding this option before signing an agreement. For example, ask what the average time frame is for concluding an investigation. Know that in many states if you refuse to close voluntarily during an investigation, the alternative may be an immediate Emergency Suspension. Please keep in mind that if you surrender your license (not inactivate but surrender) in some states, you relinquish your right to appeal.

Get Reliable Advice Prior to Making Any Major Decisions

Depending on the size of your program or the severity of the allegations, you may want to consult an attorney. As noted, if you have been informed of a law enforcement referral, it is recommended that you seek legal advice as quickly as possible. You should also obtain information about your ability to use an advocate or consultant. If you are a union member, contact your union immediately. No matter how dire the situation may appear, give yourself time to consider your options. Understand that providers can be vindicated through investigation. They also can and do win appeals. Seek reliable advice. Any decision you make should be an informed decision. Do not rely solely on your licensing representatives for recommendations or advice.

AFTER AN INVESTIGATION

At the conclusion of an investigation, you may be given the option of complying with a formal agreement rather than having legal action taken against your license. Frequently agreements are time limited and correspond with a predetermined probationary period. Agreements often include sanctions such as reduced quota, frozen enrollment, age restrictions, consultation with a mentor, additional staff, or additional and specific training requirements. Some states attach fines to negotiated agreements. If a formal agreement is presented as an option, consider the following:

- If you are asked to meet with representatives from your licensing authority, try to take someone with you who can provide informed support. If you are a union member, contact your union for assistance.
- Do your homework and collect information before you need it. What do agreements generally look like in your state? If you do sign, are you subject to an increased number of unannounced visits, for example?
- Take responsibility as warranted. If your intention is to negotiate a workable agreement, an automatic denial of any personal responsibility for what occurred, especially if untrue, is not a good plan. If you

acknowledge there may be issues that need correction, demonstrate what you have already corrected and how you propose to make future corrections.

- Consider your bottom line. Signing an agreement can be tempting, especially if you have been closed and you're told that by signing you can reopen your program. However, make sure you are not signing something you can't live with. For example, consider what type of potential income reduction you can realistically absorb and still stay in business. In most instances your licensing authority will periodically check to make sure that you are adhering to your agreement. This often means an increased number of unannounced visits.
- Before you sign anything, make sure you understand everything your agreement contains. Often an agreement includes a stipulation requiring you to relinquish your right to appeal if you are found to be in violation of your agreement. Relinquishing the right to appeal is a major concession; try to avoid it. Ask questions. For example, is the agreement time limited? Is it automatically rescinded, or does your agency periodically reevaluate?
- Don't take a passive role when the future of your business is at stake— come prepared to negotiate. The word *agreement* implies two or more parties have reached a consensus. Your regulatory authority may have oversight, but you need to remember that as a licensed provider you do have rights.
- Always give yourself sufficient time to consider all your options before signing an agreement. Don't allow yourself to feel pressured. Ask questions and get reliable advice.

IV. The Appeals Process

If after an investigation a licensing agency or another empowered authority (a social service agency, for example) determines sufficient cause to support allegations made against you or your program, one result may be legal action taken against your license. This may include Sanctions, a Refusal to Renew, Revocations, or an Emergency Suspension. In some states a final determination of abuse or neglect by a social service agency may result in the immediate suspension of your license by your regulatory agency. For most providers, receiving this type of notification is traumatic. Take a deep breath and evaluate your current situation. Seek reliable, objective assistance in determining how you should proceed. Do not rely solely on your regulatory authority to explain your options.

If after serious consideration you conclude the agency's determination is based on incomplete or inaccurate information, you should strongly consider appealing the decision. Note that in many states an appeal hearing is specifically focused on whether the agency making the final determination did so in agreement with its own agency policies and procedures. For that reason it is critical for you to have an organized record of what actually occurred during the investigation.

In most instances, any legal order you receive should contain instructions about your right to appeal. Carefully read any communication regarding your investigation as soon as you receive it. In making your decision, even if you determine you don't want to continue operating your child care business, make sure you fully understand the potential consequences of an unchallenged license revocation or suspension. For example, if you choose to return to early child care at some future date, will your license revocation affect your ability to reapply?

Most states have a deadline for filing an appeal. If you miss the date to file, you may miss your opportunity. So if you feel the agency's decision is based on inaccuracies or if you can demonstrate that an agency did not follow their own rules and procedures when making their decision, file your appeal as quickly as possible. Usually you will receive a response to your request within a few weeks. The agency response will include a date, time, and location for your appeal hearing. Do not neglect to follow up if you don't receive a timely response. Send your appeal request in a way that allows you to track and confirm delivery. If the initial revocation or suspension you receive does not include appeal information, contact the agency immediately and request instructions about how and where to file.

Some providers decide to represent themselves at their appeal hearing. I would suggest before making that decision that you familiarize yourself with how the appeal process works in your state. Do you appear in person before a magistrate or hearing officer, for example? If you are a union member, find out what type of representation or resources the union offers. Understand who is responsible for translation, if needed. Check your insurance coverage to determine whether the insurance company provides representation. If you've done your homework, you may already have the names of attorneys or advocates who have experience with this process. If at all possible, talk with other providers who have been through this. Having the most accurate information possible will help you make informed decisions and increase your chances of a successful appeal.

Usually the agency responsible for supporting the allegations will be allowed to present their case before you present your defense to the hearing officer or magistrate. Agency representatives will present evidence they believe justifies their support of allegations made against you. Sitting in an appeal hearing and listening to disparaging remarks about you and your program can be disheartening. At those moments keep in mind that you are there to present your perspective. Be prepared to submit evidence that supports your position. Maintain a calm demeanor at all times.

- The first step is to make a list of individuals who can provide relevant testimony on your behalf. Often the number of people who can provide in-person testimony at an appeal hearing is limited. Choose carefully; you want people who have actually seen the operation of your program. Ask people who are reliable and will show up when they tell you they will. Most importantly, choose people who will not offer any surprises during testimony. Make sure that if you use a representative, they have access to your witnesses prior to the hearing. Don't ask anyone to testify if you do not know how they will respond when questioned. In the majority of instances, everyone testifying will be under oath. Never expect or request that someone lie on your behalf.
- Written testimony is usually accepted. Some states limit how many references can be submitted. Make sure references are sent directly to you

or your representative and not directly to the hearing officer. You want the opportunity to review any information before it's submitted.

- Depending on the specifics of your case, you may want to submit other items on your own behalf. This is when copies of Family Surveys, Monitoring Visit Logs, targeted information in your Policy Manual, copies of previous visit reports, and copies of relevant regulations can all work to your advantage. Depending on the specifics of the supported allegations, copies of child care records, emails, texts, photographs, documentation, and attendance records may also be helpful. Organize and label your submissions carefully. Check for any inconsistencies or inaccuracies prior to submitting anything.

- Request a copy of the investigation report and any other relevant evidence (police reports, photographs, witness statements, and so on) used to support an agency's determination. Make sure you request all the case material when you file your request for appeal so you and/or your representative will have the opportunity to review it before your hearing.

- Although an appeal hearing is not intended to be a personal attack, there are times when specific allegations may appear very personal. Allowing yourself to engage in retaliatory personal attacks or get caught up in emotional exchanges can swiftly derail your case. You need to maintain your composure and act professionally at all times.

- As a small business owner, one of the most important ways you can protect and sustain your business is to do your homework. It's never too late to start collecting necessary information. Before making any important decisions, collect as much information as possible. Don't handicap yourself by being too embarrassed, too shy, or too fearful to reach out to people who can help you. Help is available, and you might be surprised by the number of providers who are vindicated at appeal hearings.

V. Allegations of Abuse and Neglect

If you, someone working in your program, or someone in your household is accused of abusing or neglecting a child, seek reliable advice immediately. If it's a household member who does not work in your program, in most states you are still required to self-report to your licensing agency. Make sure you understand the requirements in your state. In some states any allegation of abuse and neglect, not a finding, is sufficient to close your program. Operating your business in a proactive way can help protect you. You may not have control over whether someone makes an allegation; however, you do have control over the procedures and policies you implement to protect children and to protect your business. Understand that if an allegation of abuse and neglect is supported, in most states that information may automatically disqualify you from possessing an early child care license. Make sure you understand the consequences of a supported allegation as well as all options available to you.

If a false or inaccurate allegation is made, it's your preparation and knowledge that can make a difference in whether you will continue to operate your program. Good preparation, not paranoia, will help you protect your business. Regardless of the state in which you operate your business, the consequences for a provider who is alleged to have nonaccidentally injured or neglected a child can be very serious. Allegations of abuse and neglect in many states are investigated by a designated social service agency, such as the Department of Children and Families, Child Protective Services, or Department of Social Services. In other states the agency responsible for the investigation of abuse and neglect allegations may be the same agency responsible for the licensure of your program—know which agencies are responsible for which oversight. In instances when a separate agency is responsible for oversight, it is common to see joint investigations (such as with social services and licensing).

POLICIES AND PROCEDURES

The nature of your profession makes you vulnerable to all types of complaints. In the majority of cases, it is not sufficient for a provider to rely solely on their assertion that nothing inappropriate occurred. Consistent disclosure from an affected child, regardless of age or lack of corroborating witnesses, usually holds a great deal of weight during an investigation or subsequent hearing. This often occurs regardless of a provider's years of experience or the number of positive references written on their behalf. Take a good look at the daily operation of your program and incorporate routines and policies that allow you to demonstrate, if needed, why an inappropriate incident *could not* have occurred. This is especially true if the allegations against you involve an infant or preverbal child. Clearly written policies and procedures that identify your behavior management, supervision, bathroom, and napping policies, which you can easily share with client families and investigators, can help you protect your business.

Employing good strategies in the management of children's behavior can certainly make your job easier. The more effective tools and age-appropriate strategies you have at your disposal should work to your advantage. The majority of states have regulatory language that specifies which types of behavior management can never be employed while operating an early child care program. Carefully read and understand the regulations and policies governing behavior management. Also understand that in some states, corporal punishment of your own children (or any child) alleged to be committed by you or a household member who does or does not work in your program, can adversely affect your child care license. If corporal punishment is administered in the presence of child care children, if corporal punishment of a child is illegal in your state, and/or if the type or frequency of the punishment can be reasonably perceived as abuse, all of these examples can affect your ability to maintain a license. Do not assume anything! It's to your benefit to have a behavior management policy specific to your program that reflects the ages and developmental stages of children currently enrolled, inclusive of your state's behavior management requirements. Once parents/guardians have had the opportunity to read your policy, request their signature acknowledging their understanding. In addition to parents/guardians, any staff, household members, volunteers, or assistants should have a clear understanding of your program's behavior management policy. Require their signatures as well.

Your understanding of your state's supervision regulations, as well as policies clarifying those regulations, plays an important role in avoiding accusations of neglect. If, for example, a child leaves your program unnoticed, the first question is always, "Where were you?" The final determination of fault usually comes down to whether you were appropriately adhering to all of your state's supervision requirements. Any safeguards over and above what's required in regulations (such as a bell on your door that alerts you if a child is leaving the premises, cameras, or alarm systems) can help in defending against allegations of neglect.

Unfortunately, unintended events *do* occur, even with additional safeguards in place. Document everything leading up to the incident while it is fresh in your mind. If one child injures another child, the question of "Where were you?" and how quickly you were able to intervene will be important. If a child leaves your program unnoticed, how quickly the absence is noted, as well as how quickly the child is returned and by whom, will influence the final determination of any subsequent investigation. Be proactive in how you document and how you supervise. If you employ staff, consider ways to reinforce the necessity for consistent supervision by introducing policies such as restricting cell phone use during child care hours. Remember that you are responsible for your staff. If a staff member is found to have used inappropriate behavior management techniques or was not supervising children appropriately, you could easily be found negligent even though you were not directly involved in the incident. Providers sometimes feel that because there have been no allegations in the past, there will be no allegations in the future. Do not leave the future success of your business to luck.

INJURIES

Regardless of how well you supervise, at times one child will injure another child or a child will accidentally fall or be injured. Always document any incident that involves the injury of a child while in your care. Create your documentation while the incident is fresh in your mind. Notify families of the incident, provide them with a copy of your documentation, and request that they sign and date a copy of any material you share with them. Your regulations, as well as the severity of the injury or incident, will dictate whether you immediately notify a parent/guardian or whether it can wait until pickup time. Double-check to make sure you understand any additional requirements. For example, under what circumstances are you required to contact your licensor in addition to contacting a parent/guardian?

Do not make the mistake of procrastinating to the point that a parent/guardian brings the incident to your attention before you bring it to theirs. I have seen instances when providers think they don't want to start trouble so they don't notify the family, in the hopes a child will not disclose or the injury will go unnoticed. This is not a good business plan. Most states require providers to create an Incident/Injury Report when something occurs. Using this form appropriately and adhering to all regulatory requirements can provide some protection.

I sometimes meet with providers who feel it's not in their best interest to keep a written account of injuries. They feel that keeping a written record will allow people with a negative agenda to use this information against them. Actually the opposite is true. Keeping a record provides you with an opportunity to clearly describe from your perspective what occurred. Don't provide other individuals the opportunity to speculate or make assumptions about the events that you have firsthand knowledge of.

Similar to the Incident/Injury Report, many states require that you create an Observation Report if you see an unexplained injury. Any unexplained injury or dramatic mood swing you observe should be followed by a discussion with affected parents/guardians. Make sure you document what you see as quickly as possible. Also document any explanation you are given. Ask parents/guardians to sign and date your documentation. If you decide to record conversations or use photographs to illustrate what you've observed, make sure you check the laws in your state and obtain any necessary permissions. If you have concerns regarding the reliability of what you're told, contact your licensor. Make sure you understand the requirements for reporting suspicions of abuse and neglect in your state. Sometimes a parent/guardian who is being questioned regarding allegations of abuse and neglect may attempt to deflect accusations by redirecting attention to their early child care provider. Sometimes this situation can occur when there are no corroborating witnesses or when the child is preverbal and unable to give testimony. Under these circumstances, your organized documentation takes on special importance.

YOUR IMAGE AND TEMPERAMENT

What about you, and what people think about you? Temperament is important in child care. Working with children is hard work. The idea that children are always cooperative, sweet, passive, and easily engaged and motivated is nonsense. Your temperament when working with children can be a major factor in the success and protection of your business. Think about what image you project to families, children, and the other professionals you are required to interact with. Unfortunately, it is much easier to believe an allegation, whether true or not, when it involves an individual who appears to be consistently defensive, intimidating, or angry. Children in your care should never be afraid of you—intimidation is never a legitimate behavior management strategy. Don't sabotage your business by giving clients or children reason to believe you or someone working with you could intentionally injure or neglect a child.

VI. Questions from the Field

The following are real questions I've received from providers who found themselves in trouble.

> I recently had allegations made against my program. I have been a licensed provider in good standing for a long time. When I looked to my licensor (who knows my program) and my resource and referral agency (R&R) coordinator (who monitors my program regularly) for support, all I received was a cold shoulder. I felt angry and betrayed. What is the purpose of working hard to maintain an excellent licensing history when it appears to carry no influence when something unexpected occurs?

Providers feel that a good or even excellent licensing history should at the very least give them the benefit of the doubt when allegations are made against them. Learning that the professionals who know firsthand about your commitment to early child care are unable or unwilling to provide support can be disheartening.

Licensing and state social service agencies often have little or no control over how they respond to allegations made against an early child care program. Most state agencies are required to investigate all credible allegations. Because of this, it might appear that your licensing history has no relevance. While it may not be relevant at the time of intake, it can certainly have relevance during an investigation. Licensors and investigators usually review a provider's licensing history as part of their investigation. A positive licensing history can go a long way in setting the tone for what comes next.

Also, keep in mind that while a licensor or a representative of an R&R or network may be restricted from providing references or public support, they may be able to provide support behind the scenes. Don't automatically burn bridges because you initially feel angry or hurt. Don't assume the professionals who are familiar with your program are not supporting you. In truth, their support, one way or another, may not influence the final determination of an investigation. Don't become distracted—focus on what you are able to do to disprove allegations as quickly and effectively as possible.

> A false allegation was made against my program recently. When the investigators came to my home, they demanded to be allowed to go through my entire house, not just the rooms that were licensed. I felt violated. A cop would need a warrant. Is this even legal?

This is an example of why it is necessary for you to understand your state's regulatory authority as it applies to your business. You really should know what they can and can't do before they show up at your front door.

Many states have changed the wording in their regulations from *licensed space* when describing your facility to *premises*. For example, in the past second-floor bedrooms not used for the direct care of children were not included on the license as *licensed space*. Generally, licensors were prohibited from going into parts of the home that were not designated as licensed space. However, in states where the word *premises* is now used to describe your environment, licensors are empowered to visit all areas of your facility, including the entire structure where your child care is housed. If you are operating in an apartment, this can apply to common areas throughout the entire building. This wording may or may not have been used when you initially applied for your license. That's why it's important to keep up-to-date with any changes made to your regulations, including not only new regulations but also the wording of existing regulations or policies. This change in wording is often in response to incidents or other concerns that have occurred in areas of an early child care environment not designated as licensed space. Many types of allegations may require an investigator or licensor to access all areas of your house or building. Find out what the regulations are in your state. Staying prepared is your best protection in situations such as this.

> I provide foster care in addition to operating a licensed family child care home. Recently an adolescent foster child was briefly placed in my home on an emergency basis. A few days after she left, I was informed that she had made a sexual abuse allegation against my husband. My child care license was suspended while an investigation was conducted. The investigators concluded that my husband did not abuse this girl. What happens now, and what stops her from doing this again?

There is no question that anyone who has a family child care license opens themselves up to a type of vulnerability that is not common in most professions. Providing foster care also invites the very real risk of increased vulnerability. Providing both family child care and foster care simultaneously requires an individual who is prepared to deal with all types of allegations. This is especially true in foster care when social service agencies are not always forthcoming with sufficient background information on foster children when searching for an available placement, especially an emergency placement. Unfortunately, I have heard variations of this story many times.

If the allegations were not supported, this should be the end of this investigation. An affected provider should be allowed to reopen their child care facility immediately. Make sure to request the final determination in writing, and keep that notification where you can easily retrieve it if this comes up again.

Because a substantial number of abuse and neglect allegations are credible, all allegations must be investigated. Understanding that fact doesn't make it any easier for individuals who are attempting to do everything appropriately and still find themselves accused. In some instances a child who is removed from one home and placed in another may disclose to a new family, school nurse, or social worker that they have been abused in the past. The specifics of the accusation may change, so it is possible for a second investigation to occur. Unfortunately, there is no guarantee that a child who makes one accusation will not make another. Many providers and their families feel this is the tipping point and conclude they don't want to continue offering child care.

I strongly recommend that if you choose to continue providing family child care that you reconsider your foster care commitment. It has been my experience in working with providers who are offering both foster care and family child care that many assume it's possible to compartmentalize these two distinctly different types of child care. It's not. If allegations are made against you or a member of your household concerning your foster care, your licensing authority will be made aware, and although nothing may be alleged against your child care program, your ability to provide early child care can be jeopardized.

BUILDING BACK BETTER

SECTION 3 LOOKS AT PRODUCTIVE WAYS to move forward after allegations, investigations, closures, and appeals. Because "Building Back Better" is the overall theme for this section of the book, in this case study we will revisit Anne from section 1 and Sarah and Tim from section 2. While it's true that many people who have been involved in licensing intervention go on to reestablish successful early child care businesses, other providers are unable to move forward after their experience.

Family child care, unlike many categories of care, is up close and personal. For many providers, licensing intervention that results in closure can be devastating. Many individuals caught up in this type of interaction take it very personally. That's why it is so important to step back and give yourself time to decide what you're going to do. Keep in mind that in most cases you do have options. Try not to make impulsive decisions before you've given yourself the opportunity to gain some perspective.

I. Case Study Three

ANNE

Although she was allowed to stay open after her initial visit with her new licensor, Anne had to attend a series of meetings at her agency's regional office.

During those meetings a potential probationary period was discussed as well as sanctions that could be imposed. Needless to say, Anne was incredibly confused and frightened. Because Anne was a union member, after the initial meeting with her licensing agency, she finally found the courage to call her union. Anne had delayed making the call because she was embarrassed, and she still could not believe that she was in this situation. (Regardless of whether you have a union affiliation, you should seek reliable support.)

With support from her union representative, Anne was able to continue to operate her child care program. However, Anne was required to make concessions. Anne had to attend a second safe sleep training. Her enrollment was frozen at six children, and she needed to employ a mentor for six months to provide support and instruction. Anne felt the requirement to hire a mentor was especially humiliating. Anne decided to close her program for two weeks so she could think about whether she really wanted to sign her agreement. Some of the families who were aware that something was going on withdrew their children. Anne was forced to terminate her contract with her assistant and postpone any thoughts of increasing her enrollment.

During her closure, Anne talked with her family and considered whether it was worth it to start all over again. That's really the way she felt. Even though she had been operating her program for eleven years, her world had suddenly been turned upside down and she felt that if she signed the agreement, it would be like starting from scratch. After much consideration Anne decided that when it came right down to it, she did love working with children and she had loved her job. She decided it was time to swallow her pride and see whether she could begin again. Anne resolved to build a new and better business. She was determined to learn from her mistakes.

Once Anne had made the decision to revitalize her program, she became focused on the changes that were necessary so that she could avoid any repetition of what occurred in the past. Although Anne continued to believe that she had not intentionally done anything wrong, she realized that, intentional or not, she had unnecessarily jeopardized her business. Anne began the process of thinking proactively rather than reactively. She began to see working with a mentor as an opportunity rather than a punishment. Anne has recovered from her troubles to remain the owner and operator of a very successful early child care business.

SARAH AND TIM

Sarah and Tim's ability to continue to provide child care survived their investigation. They were referred to a lawyer who had expertise with administrative law. Although the final determination was decided in their favor, the cost, including loss of income and attorney fees, was expensive. Their child care program was closed for approximately ninety days, and during that time most of their child care families found alternative placements. Although the majority of their child care families gave Sarah and Tim their support in their interviews with investigators, there were a lot of uncomfortable discussions with families who felt they had been disrespected when Sarah and Tim did not tell them the truth about why they were closing.

Tim felt he could no longer assist Sarah in her child care business. As a matter of fact, he was strongly against Sarah reopening her program in their home. He felt they had too much to lose. He did not want to see himself or his family placed in such a vulnerable position again. He knew he had not injured a child, but that did not stop him from thinking about what could have happened if the allegations had been supported. He still believed that people who knew about the complaint looked at him differently. He couldn't get past the fact that someone had accused him of hurting a child, and he worried that some people continued to believe those accusations.

Sarah felt torn. She liked her job, and she enjoyed owning her own business. But she often thought that perhaps if she had not had her husband assisting her, all of this might never have happened. She believed Tim would never intentionally injure a child; however, she was also beginning to believe that men working in family child care programs were more vulnerable to accusations.

Sarah attempted to reopen her business. Tim refused to be in the house when child care children were present. Sarah had always had the support of her family when operating her business. That support was no longer available. She experienced problems interviewing new families. She didn't know whether it was wise to tell them about what had occurred or whether she should avoid the whole issue unless someone raised a question. She consistently felt stressed, and she eventually decided it just wasn't worth it. Operating her business had become a burden.

I met Sarah and Tim during a workshop with a provider support group. Although Sarah was no longer operating a family child care program, both Sarah and Tim volunteered their time to work with providers who were having difficulties. They were amazing advocates. Providers appreciated their story as well as their recommendations about how to navigate the investigation process. Talking with people who had actually experienced an investigation and who were willing to share their experience allowed other providers a unique understanding of the full picture of what can occur.

DISCUSSION

I intentionally included both of these case studies because they depict different outcomes. Anne persevered and went on to successfully change her program and her outlook. She also was wise enough to give herself some time and space before making any major decisions. Now she operates a larger and more successful program than she did prior to her licensing intervention. Anne is a great example of what can happen when a small business owner decides to use the resources available to create a realistic and proactive business model.

Sarah and Tim, however, acknowledged that they felt they could not ignore the damage they believed had occurred as a result of false allegations. After some consideration of the best way to move forward, they decided to close their family child care program. Although Sarah and Tim did not choose to continue to operate their business, they did continue to advocate for the professionals in family child care. Sarah took time to consider what was best for her and her family. She even attempted to reopen her program briefly. In the end, Sarah and Tim decided to use their unpleasant experience to inform and assist other providers.

Again, these stories and these outcomes are not unusual. Staying informed, identifying reliable resources, and acknowledging potential issues allows providers to make informed decisions.

II. Goals and Objectives

Regardless of whether you are just opening your business or are returning to early child care after a hiatus or a closing due to a licensing intervention, it's a good idea to look forward in a positive way. Change is not always easy, but anyone who operates a successful business understands that being flexible and staying informed offers a clear advantage. Communities change, trends in child care change, demographics and the amount of competition can change. Operating a successful and relevant business requires providers to periodically reestablish goals and objectives.

A goal for most, if not all, individuals who open family child care businesses is to operate a profitable and successful business. To achieve that goal, it's necessary to establish and then meet a variety of objectives along the way. The following list of objectives is an example of what may be appropriate for someone returning to child care after a licensing intervention, or for anyone who wants to operate a sustainable business.

Objectives:

- To be able to operate your business in a way that helps you avoid disruptive issues with your regulatory authority.
- To create an environment that ensures the health and safety of every enrolled child.
- To acquire the necessary skills to facilitate appropriate growth and development for all children participating in your program.
- To create collaborative relationships that enhance your work environment to the benefit of everyone associated with your business.
- To develop effective business strategies that allow you to successfully market your service to ensure full enrollment.

You may have different goals and objectives. Maybe you are returning to child care or opening a child care facility because you have grandchildren who need a reliable child care placement. Maybe you want to homeschool your own children and have decided that caring for other children as well as your own will allow you the opportunity to be at home. Whatever your goal, it's helpful to identify the steps or objectives you will need to meet to achieve your goal. For example, if your goal is to homeschool, identify what you need to earn to achieve your goal of being able to stay at home, which will help you determine your enrollment objectives. In this example, identifying your overhead would be a necessary objective. Itemizing realistic objectives that will allow you to achieve your goal is an important first step.

III. Where to Go from Here

Between the COVID-19 pandemic and the expansion of universal preschool in some parts of the country to include two- and three-year-olds, the first few years of the 2020s have been especially difficult for family child care providers. Many providers were forced to close due to COVID. Other providers have had negative experiences with their state agencies and have chosen or been forced to close their programs during investigations or appeals. Providers are leaving the profession in droves, while simultaneously the demand for child care has never been higher. Family child care providers have been continually forced to react to change, and it's easy to understand why they are concerned about the future of their profession. The narrative for early child care is now more frequently defined by individuals who are not providers or the families of children in early child care programs. Yet, despite all this, many providers see this as a time of opportunity and are looking forward to the future.

Revitalizing and rebuilding involves evaluating where you're at and then determining where you'd like to be. Evaluating your current status means asking yourself some important questions. For example, are you generating enough profit to make it worthwhile for you to stay in business? Are families leaving because children are aging out, or are they leaving for other placements? Are you happy doing the work you're doing? These are all very basic questions when deciding whether you want to continue to operate your business. Revitalizing an existing business involves making any necessary changes that will improve your potential for success. Remember that it's *your* business. Despite what licensors, inspectors, monitors, politicians, accreditation specialists, and trainers may tell you, it's still your business. As a small business owner who pays taxes and makes a considerable contribution to the common good, you do have a say in how you operate your program.

I have spoken to too many providers who have lost confidence in how they can and should operate their programs. So often family child care providers are made to feel that whatever they do, it never seems to be good enough. Family child care has somehow become the ugly stepchild in some imaginary early child care hierarchy. Many family child care providers have turned themselves and their homes inside out in an attempt to demonstrate that they provide quality child care, without any clear understanding of what "quality child care" actually means. Who is the arbiter of quality, and is the definition real or imaginary? As a licensor for twenty years, I visited thousands of early child care programs. I visited programs operated by individuals who had master's degrees in early childhood education. I also visited programs where the providers had GEDs. Based on my experience, the quality of care was not determined by the degree, the neighborhood, the category of care, or the race or ethnicity of the provider. It has always been my opinion that, ultimately, the quality of any early child care program is determined by the positive results observed in participating children as well as the level of satisfaction of their families.

No one teaches children how to grow, nor do we teach them how to develop. No curriculum allows us to implement that type of instruction. Instead, an internal process fosters growth and development naturally, whether or not children are enrolled in an early child care facility. Having said that, when given the opportunity, skilled early child care providers facilitate healthy growth and development in every interaction they have with young children. This occurs when they hold them, feed them, change their diapers, and eventually when they participate in their activities and discussions. Providers are not parents/guardians but rather professional caregivers. Good providers find ways to promote specific skill development that correlates with each child's individual pace of development and aptitude.

This type of facilitation and personalized enhancement is more easily accomplished in smaller groups. Family child care offers an intimacy that enhances understanding of each child through continuity of care. This allows providers to create meaningful bonds with children. Like good parenting, good family child care provides the opportunity for healthy social and emotional development. Generally, family child care programs provide an environment in which each child is recognized as an individual with specific needs and with their own unique developmental benchmarks. If family child care is your chosen profession, you should feel proud of your choice. If you feel that you want to revitalize, rebuild, or open a family child care business, it is important that you feel confident in your decision and in the category of care you have chosen.

If you find yourself at a crossroads in your business, please consider the following:

- Do you like kids? I rarely hear that question asked. One would think it is the most important question for anyone thinking about working in this profession. Despite that, I have never seen it asked on a licensing application, and it is not usually a question asked by licensors, inspectors, or monitors. Not every person enjoys working with children. It is generally not something that can be taught or quantified. Children, like adults, can be difficult to deal with. You may not love every child enrolled in your program, but you should enjoy working with them. Anyone choosing this profession needs to take a good, long look in the mirror. There may be many advantages to operating a home-based business, but if you do not have a natural affinity for children, it can create real challenges when you attempt to sell your service. Well-informed people who take the time to ask this question are generally the people who go on to develop and operate successful family child care programs.
- Evaluate your environment. You are selling a service that includes the nurturing and care of children. In many ways your space will dictate how you operate your program. You may have a thousand creative ideas, but if your physical environment cannot simultaneously support your ideas while also supporting the quality of your home life, your program may not succeed. Critically assess your environment to determine what is realistically possible. If there is a disconnect, look for available resources (parks, museums, and so on).
- In states where universal pre-K is available, providers who have met the criteria for entry into this program often share that families appear

disappointed when they find they have received a referral to a family child care program rather than a center. Try to remember that if a client feels they prefer center-based care to family child care, your job is not to convince them that somehow you have replicated a center but rather to demonstrate why home-based care may be a better option for their child. You can't do that effectively if you don't believe in the type of care you provide.

Often when a provider is vindicated through investigation or hearing, no formal apologies are given. Providers do not receive a letter in the mail saying, "Sorry for the inconvenience." Rarely does any private or public acknowledgment occur when a provider is vindicated through investigation or receives a reversal of a negative decision at their appeal hearing. Most states do not reimburse for time lost. When Tim shares his experience with other providers, he tells them how bitter he still feels. The investigation caused real trauma for him and his wife, and he explains that it is difficult to get past what occurred because there was no real closure. The assumption often seems to be that if a provider is allowed to reopen, that should be sufficient, and any further expectation is unrealistic. For many providers who have had similar experiences, it often seems not enough, and simply being allowed to reopen does not fix things.

Sarah shared that in considering whether to close her family child care, she realized she could not continue to operate her program and pretend that nothing had happened. She found herself feeling defensive and angry. She also shared that she was a lot less trustful. When she interviewed new clients, she couldn't help but think that this might be yet another person who could file a complaint. After serious consideration, Sarah and Tim determined that their experience had affected them in ways they had not anticipated, even though they had been allowed to reopen their program. Wisely, after serious consideration, they acknowledged they were not able to reintroduce the positive energy that had previously allowed them to operate a successful program. Acknowledging how you feel and understanding how it may influence the future operation of your business is important.

As a consultant, I have a variety of contracts. One of my contracts includes an obligation to represent providers who have chosen to appeal negative agency decisions. I candidly admit that this is my most challenging professional responsibility. The consequences of losing an appeal for many providers seems catastrophic. Many of the individuals I represent are heads of household who rely on their child care businesses for their financial survival. Sarah and Tim were fortunate in that they could decide to close and still pay the bills. Tim may have felt bitter about being falsely accused, but they did have options. The majority of providers I have represented have fortunately had their decisions reversed, but many of these providers who were forced to find other jobs while waiting for a decision opted not to reopen their programs. The decision to reopen is not always easy. Once a provider experiences a prolonged investigation and appeal process, which can sometimes take months, it's difficult to make the decision to start over. It is not unusual for providers who have gone through this to experience periods of depression. Devoting your career to the care of children and then being falsely accused can be devastating.

I have also represented providers who did not get a reversal of their negative decision. Although most states offer the option to initiate a second appeal in Superior Court, my experience shows that most providers ultimately sadly decide to walk away. When deciding whether to revitalize and rebuild your business after licensing intervention has caused you to close, there are additional considerations:

- Anne chose to use this period of closure as an opportunity to reinvent her business. In many ways she was fortunate that she was able to do this. For many providers it is not so easy to start all over again. Cash flow and access to financial support is important when revitalizing and rebuilding your business. As a child care provider and small business owner, you may be eligible for local grants or subsidies. Check with your local office of the Small Business Association, as well as local, state, and federal websites, to see what type of support is available. Talk with your bank as well as family and friends.

- If you are feeling dazed and demoralized by your experience and you are deciding to reopen because you feel you have no other choice, that is not always the best way to begin. Carefully consider your options. Are there other viable job opportunities you may want to consider?
- Often, after a provider has been successful in an appeal process and reopens their business, a period of increased scrutiny follows. You may find yourself receiving an increased number of unannounced visits. This is especially true if your initial licensing intervention was based on allegations of over-enrollment or lack of supervision. Will you be able to accept that an increased number of unannounced visits may simply be a normal part of regulatory oversight, or based on your experience, are you going to take every licensing interaction personally?
- It is rare for a licensor to be transferred or removed in response to a provider's request. You could very well be dealing with the same licensor you were interacting with when your licensing intervention occurred. Can you face that?
- Peer relationships can also fall victim to licensing intervention. If you were part of a network or support group, you may find your previous arrangement was terminated while you were closed. Some providers harbor resentment against people they feel should have been more supportive during their closure. As a result, they can become more isolated. You want your new beginning to be as positive as possible. Isolation does not help in reestablishing a business.
- Revitalizing and rebuilding after a mandated closure is not easy—make sure that you are reopening for the right reasons. Your positive energy and your ability to get past what has occurred will be essential. Make sure you identify all the available resources in your community. Reach out to other providers who are operating successful programs. Don't make assumptions about what other people think. You may be pleasantly surprised at how willing other providers are to help. Don't be afraid to think out of the box. One of the greatest advantages in operating a small business is your ability to be flexible and to change things up when necessary.

IV. Rebuilding Enrollment and Creating a Better Program

Many providers who have been closed for any number of reasons may find it difficult to rebuild enrollment once they reopen. For providers who were closed as a result of a licensing intervention, the challenges may seem insurmountable.

If you are reopening your program, consider Anne's example. Many types of businesses periodically close for "renovation." If you're smart, like Anne, use your closure as an opportunity to make positive changes. Anne did her homework and, as a result, approached reopening her program from a positive perspective. She acknowledged there had been problems. She did a serious analysis of what she wanted to change and what her goals and objectives were. She took a close look at what was changing with child care in her community. Anne wanted to operate a profitable business and also wanted to operate her program in a way that allowed her to open her doors each morning without worrying about whether she would receive an unannounced visit. She wanted to offer a safe and appropriate child care service that reflected what the people in her community were looking for.

Anne took a good look not only at her regulations and any past mistakes she made but also at her environment. She realized that when she closed and actually had time to look around, her environment had not changed for a very long time. Anne decided to clean house. She chose her equipment and materials more selectively than she had in the past. She created a better storage and recycling system, and she focused a lot of attention on her outdoor space. When Anne reopened her business, she felt revitalized, and as she interviewed new clients, she was very effective at sharing her vision for her new and improved program.

Anne knew some people might question enrolling their children in a program that had been closed and then reopened. Anne developed a strategy to deal with potential clients who had concerns. With help from her mentor, she developed a plan to engage with clients in a truthful and forthright manner. She frequently took the initiative to explain to any potential clients that she had closed her program so that she could reopen a better business. Anne's enthusiasm and positive energy, as well as her willingness to share what she had learned from her years of experience, both good and bad, worked well for her. Her potential clients, for the most part, appreciated her honesty and candor as well as her positive energy. Anne was able to move forward in a very productive way!

CUSTOMIZE FOR YOUR COMMUNITY

Before you open or reopen your doors, make sure you understand your community. Do your goals and objectives for the type of service you want to sell coincide with what people in your community are prepared to purchase? It's difficult to conceptualize your business model in a vacuum. Many providers create a concept for their program without true consideration of their competition and the realities of their business. For example, if you have always dreamed of opening a preschool and there's a public school two blocks from your home offering free preschool, can you realistically compete?

Social media has become a successful way for many providers to attract business, but it is certainly not the only method to attract potential clients. Networking in your community is so important. Schools, religious organizations, and social groups are all good places to get the word out. Let people in your community know you are open for business. If you have adult children or other relatives who have friends who are having children, don't be shy about sharing your business card. Most important, listen to what people are asking for. Some providers find success by creating informational brochures they can drop off in mailboxes throughout their neighborhood or city.

Here are some additional steps you might take:

- Advertise online on Google, Facebook, or similar platforms.
- Create a free listing on directory websites like Yelp or Google Maps. Make sure you provide as much information as possible so your business will look good when compared to the competition.
- Create a website. If a client is considering your business, having a website helps legitimize your service.
- Create a social media page such as Facebook or Instagram for your business and begin sharing content.

- If your budget allows, create paid social media ads. Sometimes spending under a hundred dollars could be enough to reach thousands of clients in your area.

Providers frequently contact me and share information about their programs. Family child care providers all over the United States are making innovative changes in order to sustain successful businesses. An increasing number of providers believe that rather than developing a rigid formula for the type of program they want to develop, it's actually helpful to take a more flexible approach. They often begin by looking at the types of services they are prepared to offer that will most effectively accommodate their pool of potential clients. Many providers acknowledge that over time they painted themselves into a corner with the expectation that clients would always be willing to accommodate their model of care. A growing consensus among family child care providers I have spoken with suggests that understanding what people are looking for and then attempting to accommodate the needs of children and families in their communities is a more effective approach. I heard from a provider recently who had begun a membership model for a predetermined number of families. A membership includes a monthly or yearly fee, and the service replicates in some ways what was traditionally called a drop-off service. Families pay an hourly rate and must use a minimum number of hours. The provider is licensed and adheres to all regulatory requirements, including quota and ratio. Hours of operation can vary. Families complete all required forms and permissions at the time of signing their membership agreements. Schedules are created a week prior to care, and often families talk with one another to avoid potential conflicts. The provider could not be happier. She operated a traditional program for eighteen years and now generates a larger income operating a nontraditional program while working fewer hours.

Other providers have contacted me to share that although in the past they were hesitant or opposed to enrolling infants, many of them are now operating infant-only programs. Many started doing this because the large majority of calls they received for new enrollment were calls for infant care. These providers decided to follow the demand. Many of them have shared how they love the type of care they're providing.

I have also heard from providers in states such as New York where there are state initiatives for 4K and 3K programs (these programs provide free or subsidized care for three- and four-year-olds). Providers have contacted me to tell me about families who have transferred their children from programs located in public schools to family child care environments, expressing their preference for smaller group size and less intimidating environments. That type of feedback can be valuable to providers when marketing the advantages of their category of child care.

In many states, providers may request variances to better accommodate a family's needs. A variance does not waive a regulation; instead, it's an acknowledgment that there may be more than one way to meet the intent of a regulation. For example, some states have regulations that restrict the number of hours providers can offer care in a twenty-four-hour period. During and after COVID, the need for providers who could provide care during nontraditional hours increased significantly. In my state, providers were successful in submitting variance requests that allowed them to extend their day to meet this need. Providers were able to demonstrate that they could continue to maintain a healthy and safe environment. Providers in many states have used the variance process to make available a variety of accommodations for children and families. If you want more information about the opportunities for variances or waivers in your state, contact your licensing authority.

SHARE THE VALUE OF INDIVIDUALIZED CARE AND ASSESSMENTS

The value of having a provider who closely observes each child as they grow and develop cannot be overstated. As a family child care provider, you have an opportunity to create a business that is unique and personalized, one that meets the needs of participating children. Because of the comparatively small group size, the ability to provide care for multiage children, and the opportunity to get to know and understand each child, family child care offers the potential for incredible advantages to children and families. Tell that story. Having a manageable-sized program allows you the opportunity to be flexible, to adjust and accommodate when necessary. You have benefits that are not readily available in most centers or institutionalized settings.

The advantage for family child care providers to observe ongoing development in children may have long-term benefits. The Associated Press Education Team published a story on May 17, 2023, titled "Mississippi Miracle: Kids' Reading Scores Have Soared in Deep South." It appears one of the reasons given for these improved scores is that children who need it are receiving intervention earlier than in the past. This is happening, in part, because of experienced providers—providers who through their organized observations have become in many instances the catalysts for early intervention.

Most providers understand that the best way to know how a child is responding to your program is through your informal observation. Consistently evaluating and adjusting their routines to meet the developmental needs of each child is something skilled providers do on a daily basis. They introduce activities or change the environment to promote specific types of development such as crawling and walking. Because family child care usually has a smaller group size, less staff turnover, and the advantage of continuity of care, these providers have a unique opportunity to implement effective developmental assessment.

More states are now requiring that assessments (or progress reports) be conducted in early child care programs. For many family child care providers, attempting to transition from what they've always done informally to a more comprehensive written assessment can prove challenging. It's one thing to informally observe children, and then, when necessary, adjust your environment or daily activities. It's another thing to maintain a well-organized written chronology of each child's ongoing development that acknowledges all the important things you see and hear every day. This type of documentation might initially seem like a burden, but it can be an opportunity.

Let families know the advantages of assessment and how assessments are used in family child care. Sharing your assessment procedure when meeting prospective clients can provide you with a wonderful marketing tool. As we've discussed, early child care can be a very competitive profession. Your clients have the right to assume that the licensed child care setting they choose is a healthy and safe place. In addition to health and safety, most families want to know that the child care program they've chosen supports their child's healthy development. When meeting with prospective families, sharing your assessment procedure gives you a professional way to demonstrate your commitment to children's healthy overall early development. (Many assessment tools are available to help you organize your daily observations. Look around until you find one that most comfortably suits your needs.) You can demonstrate how using your assessment information allows you to introduce a well-planned schedule of daily activities to promote personalized skill development. In addition, when you share developmental indicator information (benchmarks), you help educate parents/guardians about realistic and age-appropriate goals for their children. Sharing your assessment procedure helps you establish an important communication link and shows how you value collaboration.

Here are other advantages in conducting organized assessments:

- Using an assessment tool provides you with an organized and easy way to track each child's progress and ensure that important early childhood developmental milestones are not ignored or overlooked.
- Incorporating an assessment tool into your program's offerings enables you to take a developmental snapshot that captures each child's developmental progress at a specific point in time.
- Obtaining useful information about each child's developmental level allows you to establish developmental goals and then introduce activities designed to support those goals.
- Implementing an assessment system assists in providing timely information about any areas of possible developmental delay.
- Reviewing assessment information helps you determine whether your daily activities and routines actually meet the needs of all the children in the program.
- Using an assessment tool enables you to provide materials and equipment that best support the development of children currently enrolled.
- Adopting an assessment tool provides you with a professional and organized way to share your observations with families and other professionals when indicated.

Assessments are a key tool in communicating with families—and good communication is foundational to keeping families enrolled in your program. When sharing information about developmental assessment, be clear about your role. Help your clients understand that you are not diagnosing or judging children. Explain how using age-appropriate developmental indicators provides a framework for your observations, and share how your assessment is a positive component of your child care. Let them know that you use your assessment to influence how you organize your activities and daily routines to best meet the needs of their children.

Allow families the opportunity to give you feedback about the information they would prefer to receive and how and when they would prefer to receive it. This will not affect your ability to conduct your assessments, but it will affect the way you share your information with families. Let parents/guardians know you are listening and willing to work together to make this process as collaborative as possible.

Remind families, as well as yourself, that the goal of using an assessment is not to force every child to develop in the same manner or at the same rate. Your assessment allows you to acknowledge how each child grows and develops in their own way. Be prepared to discuss how your assessment is not intended to make children comply with rigid expectations, but rather to help you better understand how to support each child's individual growth and development.

Talk about the potential rewards that can result by enrolling a child in a family child care that includes multiage groups of children. Because most family child care settings contain multiage groups, a provider's ability to determine each child's developmental needs takes on special importance. Since you do not have the luxury of ignoring the needs of one age group to focus on another's as you facilitate healthy growth and development, conducting assessments allows you to create individualized goals for all of your participating children. One way to dispel the myth about family child care being little more than babysitting is to discuss the ways in which your program promotes appropriate development for all the children in your care. Highlight the age of a prospective client's child. Talk about the activities and routines you have introduced to help meet the developmental goals for children of that age. Discuss how your periodic assessment allows you to develop personalized routines that are not always readily available or possible in other categories of care.

Here are some further tips for communicating with families about children's development:

- Identify child- and family-related resources, organizations, agencies that provide support, and events in your area, and share those resources with families.
- Be prepared to refer families to other professionals in your community when they express concerns regarding possible developmental delays.
- Share curriculum with families to link activities in child care with activities provided at home.

V. Focusing on Communication

Good communication is a necessary part of developing a successful early child care business. Understanding the various ways you can engage in productive communication will help you successfully convey your message. It's easier to sell people on your business when you are an effective communicator. In moving forward, your ability to communicate effectively can play a role in whether you go on to operate a sustainable business.

One of the primary ways you demonstrate your professionalism is through your face-to-face communication. Face-to-face communication allows for non-verbal cues such as body language and facial expressions to convey a message. It enables both the sender and the receiver to acquire immediate feedback about their ideas.

None of us are perfect, and often after a conversation we regret something we said. Sometimes we share more than we should, or we recognize that what we said may not have been well received or could easily be misinterpreted. There are also times when we remember what we said but have no memory of what other people said to us. When this occurs as part of a social interaction, we often have the option to correct any potential misunderstandings. Unfortunately, professional interactions do not always provide that opportunity.

When engaging in licensing interactions, it is important that you and your licensor, health inspector, or monitor can hear and understand each other.

That doesn't mean you will always agree—but it should mean that you all understand what is being said. It can be difficult to listen to information that you do not agree with or information that includes new requirements that mandate change or increase the cost of operating your business. However, you cannot adequately respond or make corrections or adjustments if you ignore the speaker or do not try to understand shared information. You need accurate and reliable information to operate your program.

For many years, one of my roles as a private consultant has been to advocate for and represent family child care providers at administrative hearings. As a result, I have come to appreciate how miscommunication can play a major role in the sequence of events that leads to negative licensing interaction. Frequently at hearings I hear statements like "She never told me that," "She must have heard incorrectly," or "That isn't what I said" from both providers and licensors who are defending their respective positions. Miscommunication is frequently used to try to absolve responsibility for incidents or issues. It's been my experience that this strategy rarely works for either side.

Think about how many times you've used the words *tell* or *told* when you describe how you verbally relay information. This is called *linear communication*. The word *linear* describes a one-way interaction. It doesn't guarantee that the person you're talking to is listening or understands what you said. For example, I have often heard providers say, "I told those kids not to do that." There is often an implied message that because the children were "told," the providers fulfilled their obligation, and whatever followed was not their responsibility. Diligent caregivers understand that sometimes the telling is not enough—there needs to be follow-up. Follow-up should include an attempt on your part to determine whether your message was received and understood. One of the ways to determine whether you were heard is to listen for a response. Successful interactive communication is not passive. An interactive model of communication is a back-and-forth process that involves the exchange of ideas, messages, and information.

The following communication tips are designed to help you engage in successful professional interactions.

DO NOT MAKE ASSUMPTIONS

Often when communicating with others we respond in kind. For example, if you feel someone is not engaging in a positive way, you may respond in the same manner. If your licensor is distracted or not bringing positive energy to your interaction, it is sometimes easy to assume that it's because they have an issue with you, and it is a common response to become defensive and sometimes argumentative. Let me share a relevant story.

My late husband was fifty-one when he became ill. He spent the last five months of his life in a hospital. We had two children in college and a ten-year-old son. Our health insurance was through my state insurance, so there was no option for me to stop working at that point. My mother took care of my son after school, and each evening after visiting my son I would go to the hospital to be with my husband. Each morning, I would get up and go to work. I was a family child care licensor at that time.

I did not share my story with any of the providers I visited. I felt it would be unprofessional. In looking back, I am sure some providers hated seeing me at their door. I was tired and stressed, and there were days when I thought my head was going to explode—not a great way to begin a monitoring visit.

You can never know for certain what someone else is thinking or feeling unless that person is willing to tell you. If you automatically act on an assumption and negatively react to someone's tone or body language, you could very well misinterpret the situation and make things worse. I was fortunate that the large majority of providers I worked with were able to get past my deficiencies and help keep our visits professional and on point.

Licensors and providers can work together to communicate effectively, regardless of what may be occurring in their personal lives. It is not to your advantage to assume you know what your licensor is thinking. Your tone and body language should not simply reflect your licensor's tone and body language. Your good focus and positive energy can make a significant difference in the outcome of your visit.

It is not necessary for you and your licensor to "like" one another. It's nice if that occurs, but you should be able to engage in productive communication regardless. Creating a working relationship that allows each party to feel respected and heard is a realistic goal in licensing interactions. If you find yourself almost exclusively attempting to gain your licensor's personal approval, it's not a good plan. Getting your licensor's professional approval (positive visit logs, no or few citations) is a more appropriate objective.

MAKE LISTS

If you are a licensed early child care provider, you are going to receive periodic unannounced visits. These visits are part of what you agree to when you apply for a license. Making lists of questions and potential concerns prior to a visit can improve the quality of your licensing interactions. Staying prepared allows you to feel confident about the outcome of any unannounced monitoring visits.

Maintaining an ongoing list of questions demonstrates your preparation for a visit. If you hear something about changes in regulations, if you want to make physical changes to your environment, or if you're thinking about expanding your business, ask questions. If you've heard different perspectives about quota and ratio, for example, your licensor is the person to ask. Your preparation for a visit reinforces the idea that visits can benefit you as a business owner. Anytime you can get direct answers to your questions from your licensor, it's to your benefit.

Asking questions and documenting answers also enables you to control the tempo of the visit. Often providers tell me that their participation during monitoring visits is minimal because they are rarely given the opportunity to speak unless a licensor has a question. You do have control over the amount of participation you bring to a monitoring visit. Asking questions, staying current, and allowing your licensor to understand that you want to operate a safe and successful business can produce great results.

Your licensor keeps a record of each visit. You should also be keeping a record of your understanding of what was said during the visit. When asking for your licensor's signature at the conclusion of the visit, encourage your licensor to read your material before signing. You are providing an opportunity for you and your licensor to address any potential misunderstandings. Make sure that you are given the opportunity to read anything you are asked to sign at the conclusion of a visit. Consider employing your Monitoring Visit Log for ease of use.

BREATHE, SMILE, AND TRY TO RELAX

It is remarkable how a smile and a relaxed demeanor can affect communication. It's really difficult to be negative when the person you're talking to is smiling, friendly, and relaxed. There's a quote attributed to Marshall Shelley that I love: "When attacked by a dragon, do not become one." All those old sayings like "attracting more flies with honey than vinegar" have an element of truth. You only have control over how you present. You can exercise your rights, but do it in a manner that works to your advantage.

If you are having a bad day, it's OK to acknowledge that, but it's not OK to use that as an excuse to avoid interacting with your licensor. I have seen providers use the children in their program as a distraction so they can avoid having to deal with their licensor. I have also observed licensors who never take their eyes off their checklists and never make eye contact with the provider. Both examples are unprofessional and raise red flags. When a licensor can't make eye contact, it's easy to understand why a provider may feel the licensor has a negative agenda. When a provider uses children as a distraction, it's easy for a licensor to think the provider might have something to hide.

Understand how other people perceive the message you send. This is true with licensors, child care clients, family members, and the children in your program. Body language is important, and because you are the only one who can control your body language, it's a good idea to be conscious of how you present yourself. Crossing your arms tightly in front of your body, clenching your fists, rolling your eyes, and looking everywhere other than at the person across from you all communicate a negative message. Many people are not conscious of their body language, especially when they're nervous. Your body language may convey a message that is different from what you intend. Do you demonstrate through your tone and attitude that you enjoy your work? On too many occasions I have talked with parents/guardians who complain that their provider gives them the impression the provider is doing them a favor. Don't sabotage your business by communicating that you're temperamentally unsuited for child care.

The most important element of your business is you. Trust is an enormous consideration in early child care. Like it or not, you are not simply selling your service—you are also selling yourself. How you present and interact with others goes a long way in assuring that you will continue to operate a successful business.

Your clients enter your home on a daily basis. Periodically you need to take stock of what your environment communicates about you and your business. How do you interact with your household members in the presence of clients or other professionals? Does your living environment demonstrate your good organizational skills? Do you sometimes present an overly aggressive, defensive, or argumentative posture because it's your personal space? Take the time to think about what and how you communicate with others.

OPTIMIZE EMAIL COMMUNICATIONS

Email can be used to ask questions, offer feedback, and give additional information that may not have been provided during the initial conversation. Email also allows you to get your answers in writing. I recommend that any reply to a licensing question you receive via email be printed and included in your Policy Manual.

As in all digital communication, be aware of the message you want to convey before you begin typing. Remember that email is not only a written record of your licensor's message but your message as well. Choosing this option to communicate does not mean you can say things that you would be reluctant to say in person. Keep your emails professional and on point. Although email can facilitate an interactive experience with back-and-forth, it does not provide all the benefits of in-person interactive communication.

CREATE A FAMILY CONTRACT THAT REFLECTS YOUR PROGRAM

Your Family Contract is an important form of professional communication. Like all communication, your contract needs to include clear and understandable language. A well-written contract can go a long way in helping you avoid misunderstandings and potential issues. You need to be consistent in what you say and what you do. As regulations, your enrollment, and your experience changes, so should your contract. For example, if you've had a negative experience in the past because of miscommunication, use that experience to inform your revised contract. Learn from any mistakes. It's fine to refer to samples from other programs when you are developing a contract, but make sure you create a contract that reflects the specifics of your program. Try reading your contract through the eyes of a client. Would you feel comfortable signing your contract? If your contract has not been revised in five years, there's a problem!

Consider the following as you evaluate your Family Contract:

- Try not to create separate contracts or agreements for individual families; instead, create a contract sufficiently inclusive for all your child care arrangements.
- Don't paint yourself into a corner. Some providers have been forced to increase their fees to compensate for reduced enrollment. Other providers have expanded the hours of care or the types of services they provide in order to maximize enrollment and compensation. Make sure your contract provides you with some flexibility. Let families know up front that arrangements are subject to change based on periodic evaluation.
- Educate your child care families about the difference between what you are required to do through regulation or policy and what you choose to do as an independent business owner.

In reviewing a variety of contracts over the past few years, I have found that many providers use their contracts, handbooks, policy manuals, and so forth as a substitute for ongoing in-person communication. I am frequently asked to review contracts that include twenty to thirty-five pages. I am aware that providers have been given instructions about how to create contracts that protect themselves and their programs. Protecting your business is what this book is about. However, I also get the impression that some providers feel if they put every possible contingency in writing, they can avoid not only legal or liability issues but also any personal exchanges or challenges about the way they operate their businesses. This is one of the worst examples of linear communication I can think of.

As with all types of one-way communication, you are depriving yourself of the opportunity to discover whether your clients understand or have even read your contract. Many parents/guardians have shared with me that if a contract is more than a few pages, they skim it for "the important stuff" and ignore the rest. They may sign it—in many cases because they're desperate for care—but do they agree with what it contains, and do they understand it? Who knows. As the mother of three children who were all enrolled in early child care, I would have headed for the door if my provider had handed me a thirty-five-page contract.

When you deny your client the opportunity to provide feedback or to exchange ideas or any possibility for negotiation, you are opening the door to possible resentment and passive-aggressive behavior. In achieving successful communication, soliciting feedback is always a good thing. Does that mean that you are going to comply with every request a family makes or accommodate everyone except yourself? No, it does not. What it means is that you've given the people most affected by your professional decisions the knowledge that they've been heard. You signal that you value their opinions and have used the feedback you receive when making your decisions. Providers want to know they are heard when their licensing authority is making decisions that affect them. Similarly, the people who are most affected by your decisions want to know that you are considering their opinions when establishing your rules.

Why should you care? Because it's your business! Good communication is not a one-way street. Yes, it's important that you are able to express your opinion and, when necessary, counter information you believe is false or inaccurate. It is equally important for you to really listen when exchanging information with individuals who can affect your business. It's generally when people feel ill informed that distrust and miscommunication become potential issues. Be confident in your business decisions, and do not hesitate to share information about the operation of your program in a variety of interactive ways. Try not to rely solely on your contract to convey necessary information.

VI. Creating Internal Policies

Throughout this book I have emphasized the value of learning from mistakes. Most of us want to forget about our mistakes and move on. If you are reopening after a licensing closure or a long hiatus, it's necessary to learn from the past as you move forward.

I recently consulted with a provider who had been accused of abusing and neglecting a four-month-old child. On the day the incident allegedly occurred, the parent arrived at the provider's home to pick up her child. Two hours later the parent contacted the provider demanding to know how her son's leg was bruised. The parent alleged that when she undressed the child for his bath, she saw a bruise on her child's upper thigh that appeared to be in the shape of a handprint. The provider was stunned and could not explain how that type of injury occurred. The provider denied that the injury had occurred at her home.

The parent filed a report repeating her allegations, and ultimately the case went to hearing. The provider was able to demonstrate through her internal policies and procedures the precautions she had in place to avoid this type of incident. She was vindicated at the hearing and resumed the operation of her business.

In the absence of witnesses, it is often the credibility of one individual over the credibility of another that makes the difference. Your ability to demonstrate how you operate your program using internal policies and procedures can have a positive effect. In this case, the provider had logs that she used daily. This provider's daily procedure involved a quick check at drop-off time to determine whether there were any unexplained injuries or symptoms of illness. She would enter that information in her daily log and have the parent initial the log before leaving. At the conclusion of each day at pickup time, the provider repeated the same process. In this case, the parent stated she did not see the injury when she signed the log. The magistrate, after examining a copy of the provider's logs, immediately decided in favor of the provider.

As mentioned, it's extremely important to understand your agency's regulatory policies when operating your business. It's equally important for families who have children enrolled in your program to understand *your* policies and procedures. Your policies should demonstrate how you protect the children in your program. You are required to adhere to regulatory mandates, but you can include other procedures that can protect both your program and the children you provide care for.

When reopening or revitalizing your business, review your regulations. In some states, for example, the log I just described is a regulatory requirement.

Although it was not a requirement in this provider's state, she initiated this procedure as a proactive measure. In her case it worked! If you find when reviewing your regulations that this type of log or checklist is not required, you may want to include this type of protection.

When examining how you operate your program you should not only be looking for your strengths but also—and more importantly—the areas where you are vulnerable. Anyone can file a complaint; it's frustrating to find so many providers with no protection. Creating appropriate operating procedures is not a sign of paranoia but an indicator of good business sense.

Look at the things you do daily to protect children and your business. For example, most providers have a procedure they follow when they need to use the bathroom or when they are unable to directly supervise every child. Usually these procedures include positioning children in a way that allows the provider to see and/or hear what is happening at all times. Your procedures will depend on the ages of children currently in your program. In some instances, you may employ a corral or playpen. You may have a child who you know through your experience needs additional support when you are distracted. What is your procedure for providing that support? Creating a policy specific to issues involving how you supervise demonstrates that you have formalized your business's operating procedures in a way that helps minimize any possible incidents. Does this guarantee that a child will never be hurt or injured? Unfortunately, I am not aware of anything that can make that guarantee. However, using formalized policies, procedures, checklists, or logs reinforces and demonstrates your intent to protect every enrolled child.

We discussed using a daily checklist to ensure that your environment is appropriate for children entering your program. It's easy to forget or overlook a step when you are attempting to operate a busy early child care program. Checklists and logs can help you avoid missing something. Checklists can be used in other ways as well. The log described in the case with the provider who was falsely accused of child neglect and abuse is one example. Checklists can also be valuable when you are involved in sequential behavior management strategies or when you administer first aid or medication. You can use a checklist at lunchtime when determining what and how children eat, to compile toileting information, and to ensure that you have followed all the necessary steps when you need to record an unusual observation or an injury.

Codifying this type of information in a manner that you can easily share with families and during any potential investigation gives you an advantage. Some of you reading this information are probably thinking that you already have enough to do. In truth, using checklists or logs can make your daily routine easier. It also provides the benefit of allowing you to feel more confident because you know you've checked all the appropriate boxes. Those of you who have experienced licensing intervention understand what it feels like when everything comes down to your word against someone else's. You can certainly understand the advantage this type of procedure can provide.

VII. Questions from the Field

> Information is posted on my licensing agency's website that, without context, may leave potential clients with a negative first impression about my family child care program. Is there anything I can do about this?

I have often wondered if there were a website that posted information every time a regulatory agency made a mistake, how that would be received. Unfortunately, I am not aware of any state where this occurs.

Periodically check information posted on state websites for accuracy. If the information posted is inaccurate, petition to have it removed or corrected. Be prepared to submit evidence that clearly demonstrates why the posted information is incorrect.

If the information is accurate but does not provide context, ask if you can add additional text or clarifying information (corrections that were made during the visit, for example). If that is not allowed, there are ways to mitigate some of the damage this type of posting may cause:

- Recognize that many referrals are still based on word of mouth. Talk to the families of children currently enrolled as well as past clients you have maintained a good relationship with. Without making a big deal, share any additional facts that clarify the information contained on the website. Let parents/guardians know you have nothing to hide and are only attempting to give a more accurate picture of the situation that led to the posting. By taking the initiative, you have more control over the narrative.

- Don't deny information that's true. I suggest you keep a folder handy when interviewing new clients to clarify anything that's posted on your state's website. Some states have a regulatory requirement about disclosing any previous complaints or citations to prospective clients. In those instances, make sure you understand specifically what you are required to disclose. Parents/guardians are human, and they know that everyone makes mistakes. Hearing your clarification about what's posted usually satisfies any concerns most prospective clients might have. More often than not, they will appreciate your honesty. It's also encouraging when you volunteer information rather than forcing a client to ask questions.

- Find out what your state's policy is for removing information from their website. For example, does information automatically get removed after a predetermined time? Keep in mind that because information is removed from the website, it doesn't necessarily mean that it has been redacted from your licensing history. Make sure you understand everything about how your state manages this type of information.

I have enrolled in courses to get a BA degree in early childhood education. I thought my child care families would be excited about this new initiative, but instead I have received feedback that I'm not sure I understand. One of my clients asked if that meant I was going to raise my rates. Another simply asked why I would bother. I am now beginning to wonder who I'm doing this for.

Hopefully you are continuing your education for yourself and for the children in your program! I frequently talk with providers who are enrolled in degree programs. Often those providers want to enlarge their businesses or open a center. Many states have degree requirements for making those types of changes. In states that have tiered reimbursement systems, a degree often means increased state reimbursement. Most people agree that the more knowledge you have regarding the healthy growth and development of children, the better, regardless of which category of child care you provide.

When I hear from providers about issues such as this one, many providers express disappointment and confusion regarding how their child care families perceive the service they provide. Sometimes there's a disconnect. Many families believe they are simply purchasing an available slot, which allows them to go to work and hopefully know their child is safe and happy. If you're licensed, you can accommodate their schedule, and the price is right, for some families that's more than enough. For many providers who have put time, energy, and money into developing a program that offers special educational opportunities for children, such thinking can be a major disappointment. Family child care providers frequently share feelings of disrespect and being underappreciated.

If you believe in the quality of your program, your clients will eventually see what you see. Be willing to educate your clients through your daily demonstration of what it means to provide quality care. Keep the lines of communication open. Use your assessment tool to demonstrate progress and acknowledge important bench- marks that highlight the developmental progression of participating children.

CONCLUSION

WRITING THIS BOOK has been a great pleasure for me. I believe in the value of what you do. I see family child care as the best possible conduit between home and school. In my opinion, it is the best of both worlds.

Unlike teachers in a classroom who can focus on one specific area of learning, you do not have that luxury. In early child care, *care* is often the key word in describing what you do. We sometimes underestimate how valuable the quality of that care is to the development of young minds. Tender touches, reinforcing smiles, and patient and caring direction are all very important. Those early years that children spend with you can have a dramatic effect on how they grow and develop long after they leave your program. Their self-esteem, which is so vulnerable at a young age, can be molded and nurtured by a well-suited early child care placement.

We have all heard stories about adults who participated as children in a family child care program returning years later to enroll their own children, or returning just to say hello and to let the provider know they remembered the kind care. What incredible reinforcement that provides! It demonstrates that in family child care you have the opportunity to create unique and special relationships with each child in your care.

With that degree of familiarity comes a great deal of responsibility. I have often heard providers share how frustrating it is to have so much responsibility and seemingly little or no empowerment. Many providers are often faced with the challenge of developing close relationships with children only to send them home, in the provider's opinion, to parents/guardians who may not have a clue about their own kids. A provider once described to me that the most difficult part of her job was the recognition that "all the children she cared for were not her own" and having to deal with the occasional heartbreak that occurred when she felt one of "her" kids was not given the love and attention they needed at home.

Unlike other categories of care, family child care is up close and personal. You are opening up your home and, in many cases, your heart to children from diverse backgrounds. You not only are expected to provide nurturing and attentive care to each child but also are sometimes placed in situations when you feel it's necessary to compensate for parents/guardians, or as one provider described it, to "fill in the gaps" for some of the young children in your care.

All the things you do are so important, and the variety of services you provide is sometimes underrated. It makes me furious. As a society we need you. We need your personalization and the realization that our children are not just numbers or checks at the end of the month. We need your continuity of care. We need to know there is a category of care that acknowledges that not every young child grows and develops at the exact same pace and that every child deserves patience and caring attention. Parents/guardians need to know that their child's caregiver remembers each child's name and knows their quirks and acknowledges their individual temperaments and personalities. We need you and the wonderful service you provide!

As I mentioned in my introduction, the purpose of this book is to offer assistance and encouragement to those of you who may be considering this profession. I applaud you, and I hope the information in this book will assist you as you develop your business. It was also designed for those of you who are currently licensed but may be feeling overwhelmed and considering giving it all up. If you are in that category, please reconsider. It takes a special person to do what you do. Hopefully some of what I've shared in this book will demonstrate that many providers have felt overwhelmed and then have gone on to successfully revitalize and rebuild their businesses.

For all of you, including those of you who are doing just fine, I wish that this book provides some useful assistance and protection for you and your businesses. It is my hope that family child care continues to grow and flourish. A lot of families are looking for care. All of us need to work together to make everyone understand the value of this category of care, and that starts with you. Feel proud about the type of care you provide.

When my children were young, I worked outside of my home. My reliance on my family child care provider was beyond description. I had owned and

operated a large child care center before having my children. With that experience in mind, I chose a family child care environment for all of my kids. It is
my sincere hope that as my children search for early child care for my grandchildren, family child care providers who continue to provide an often superior
and certainly special type of early child care will be available in every state.

Thank you.

RESOURCES

American Federation of State, County and Municipal Employees
www.afscme.org

Child Care Aware of America
www.childcareaware.org/providers

Child Care Resource & Referral Agency (CCR&R) Search
www.childcareaware.org/resources/ccrr-search

Child Care Technical Assistance Network
https://childcareta.acf.hhs.gov/national-resources-about-family-child-care

Council for Professional Recognition
www.cdacouncil.org/en

National Association for Family Child Care
https://nafcc.org

National Association for the Education of Young Children
www.naeyc.org

National Child Care Association
www.nationalchildcare.org

National Database of Child Care Licensing Regulations
https://licensingregulations.acf.hhs.gov

Opportunities Exchange
www.oppex.org

Service Employees International Union
www.seiu.org

INDEX